BLUEBIRD
AND THE DEAD LAKE

John Pearson is a renowned author and journalist whose
books include *The Profession of Violence*, his famous biography
of the Kray twins which won the Edgar Allan Poe Special
Award, *The Life of Ian Fleming*, *The Life of James Bond*,
The Sitwells and *Painfully Rich: The Outrageous Fortunes and
Misfortunes of the Heirs of J. Paul Getty*. His most recent book is
The Cult of Violence, a sequel to his first book on the Krays.

Richard Williams is the chief sports writer of the *Guardian*.
His books include *The Death of Ayrton Senna*, *Racers*,
Long Distance Call: Writings on Music and, most recently,
Enzo Ferrari: A Life.

Dear Sports Fan,

You have in your hands an astonishing book about one of the strangest and greatest world record attempts in history.

In 1964, in Australia's remote outback, Donald Campbell, who would later lose his life on Coniston Water, set out to drive his car at over 400 miles an hour. Things went wrong from the start, and John Pearson's classic book about Campbell is a portrait of a modern tragic hero, fighting the elements, the clock, but mostly himself.

Bluebird and the Dead Lake is one of six books that begin our Aurum classics sports list. Publishing sports writing that does justice to the story being told has always been our priority at Aurum. This new series, which covers sports ranging from cricket to boxing, rugby to baseball, gives us the opportunity to celebrate both our own books that, over the years, have come to obtain classic status, and also bring back into print neglected books that deserve to be acclaimed as such. I hope that you will enjoy them all whether you are coming to the subject, the sport, or the writer for the first time.

At Aurum Press we take great care in shaping our sports list to be as diverse and inspiring as possible and we would love to hear what you think of the classics. Let us know on twitter at #aurumsportsclassics. Every month new tweets will be entered into a draw to win a set of all the titles. You can also email me at aurumclassics@aurumpress.co.uk to find out more about our forthcoming titles.

I would also be delighted to hear your suggestions for other forgotten classics, which you think merit re-publishing for a new generation.

Yours sincerely,
Robin Harvie

July 2013

Bluebird
AND THE DEAD LAKE

The classic account of how
Donald Campbell broke the
World Land Speed Record

John Pearson

WITH AN INTRODUCTION
BY **RICHARD WILLIAMS**

This edition first published in Great Britain
2013 by Aurum Press Ltd
74–77 White Lion Street,
London N1 9PF

First published by Aurum Press in 2002
First published by Collins in 1965

A catalogue record for this book is available from the British Library.

ISBN 978 1 78131 172 1

1 3 5 7 9 10 8 6 4 2
2013 2015 2017 2016 2014

Typeset in 11.5/13.5 Granjon by J & M Typesetting, Australia

Printed and bound in Great Britain by
CPI Group (UK) Ltd, Croydon, CR0 4YY

For my grandchildren:
Ben, Brando, Edoardo, Federigo, George, Lorenzo,
Lydia, Tallulah, Tatjana and Theo

Contents

Introduction
by Richard Williams

Not until halfway through this remarkable book does the author stumble upon the central truth of his story. What he has been watching for several weeks in the middle of a salt lake in a remote part of South Australia is not simply an attempt to drive a motor car faster than one has ever been driven before. He is watching the trial of a man.

Seldom can such a trial have taken place in a more appropriately intimidating environment. As John Pearson describes it, Lake Eyre, a vast saltpan four hundred miles north of Adelaide, is a place of dust and flies, where isolated homesteads are surrounded by the bones of dead animals and abandoned machinery, where small boys catch crows in rabbit traps, where their fathers predict the weather by examining the activity of ants, and where the great white nothingness of the lake itself is swept by 'a fretful, feminine wind that kept promising to change its mind but never did'. The landscape, so precisely evoked, forms the third leading character in this drama, after the man and his car.

For Donald Campbell, destiny dealt from a stacked deck. His father, Sir Malcolm Campbell, had set records on land and water during transportation's evolutionary golden age, becoming a national hero in the process. And, as is sometimes the way of these things, the father's legacy became the son's burden. In 1964, beset by innumerable problems in his highly publicised attempt to take the world land speed record past 400 mph for the first time, Donald faced accusations that the weakest element of the enterprise was the driver himself.

'Bloody Campbell's lost his nerve,' someone mutters as the humiliations mount. Not so very long after the end of the second of two world wars, at a time when the willingness to risk life and limb carried a very different resonance, a more brutal insult could hardly have been devised. Men like Campbell, who aspired to the condition of heroism, were expected to flirt with danger, and some were expected to die. 'That's his job,' another observer asserts. 'It's always been the job of these record breakers. They all have to be willing to kill themselves, otherwise there wouldn't be any records.'

'Doubts, old boy? No, why?' Campbell, lighting a Havana cigar and mixing himself a vodka and tonic after a 300 mph run, certainly does his best to live up to the ethos enshrined in the works of Sapper, Captain W. E. Johns and Ian Fleming. But eventually he is forced to admit the reality of his plight, and from that poignant admission—and an extraordinary vision—springs a renewal of resolve.

Campbell was trying to add his name to the honour roll that began at the end of the nineteenth century, when pioneer automobilists began to battle for the title of the fastest man on land. The Comte de Chasseloup-Laubat was the first man to set the official world land speed record, recording 39.24 mph on a public road at Archères, outside Paris, in December 1898, sitting high above the fuselage of his electric-powered vehicle. His record was soon surpassed by Camille Jenatzy, an intrepid Belgian, also powered by electricity. Their contest saw the record change hands five times in little more than a year, setting a pattern of rivalry in which national prestige was among the rewards for individual success.

The great battles of the inter-war years were largely British affairs, fought between Malcolm Campbell, J. G. Parry Thomas, Henry Segrave, George Eyston and John Cobb, national heroes whose exploits made newspaper headlines. None of the drivers cut a more dashing figure than Campbell, the daredevil son of an English diamond merchant, who set his first record in 1924 at 146.14 mph in a Sunbeam on Pendine Sands in Wales, and his last in 1935, on Bonneville Salt Flats in Utah, driving one of his own Campbell Specials—all of which were christened *Bluebird*, after the popular play by Maurice Maeterlinck—at 301.13 mph. That year, aged fifty, he retired from land speed records, but he lost no time in building a boat, also called *Bluebird*, with which he broke the water speed record on Coniston Water in the Lake District, leaving it at 141.7 mph in 1939.

Sir Malcolm, as he had become, died in his sleep in 1949, aged sixty-three, a victim of ill health and bouts of depression, but his work was carried on by a son who had been both terrified and transfixed by the force of his father's personality.

Born in 1921, Donald Campbell had watched the latter part of his father's career at close quarters and felt something very like an obligation to pick up the baton. By the time John Pearson travelled to Australia to join him, the younger Campbell had established himself by setting a new water speed record of over 200 mph at Ullswater in his father's old boat, which he had fitted with a jet engine. He had also commissioned a new *Bluebird* car, again using a jet engine, but during its initial attempt on the record, at Bonneville in 1960, the car crashed at 360 mph and Campbell suffered head and neck injuries. Four years later he re-emerged in a new location with a rebuilt *Bluebird*, ready for a further attempt on a record which had assumed an almost mystical significance to him.

Pearson, then aged thirty-four, was invited to write a book about the adventure. With a biography of the naturalist Armand Denis and an award-winning first novel, *Gone to Timbuctoo*, behind him, he took leave of absence from his job at the *Sunday Times* in London, where he had been Ian Fleming's assistant on the Atticus column. He and Campbell struck up an immediate rapport, which paid dividends when the hero's supporters began to desert the project.

'It was a strange business,' Pearson reflected almost forty years later. 'I actually loved old Donald. Not many others seemed to. I was always interested in why people pursue fame. He was rather like a bullfighter—he had to keep putting his life at risk. It was frightening seeing this guy who really had lost his nerve but forced himself through sheer willpower and guts to go through with it. And he was also trying to compete with his father's image, which was a terrible thing. Afterwards he wanted me to do a book on the family, but Ian Fleming had died in 1964 and I was asked to write his biography. Later I did ghost a series for Donald in the *Sunday Express*, but I was in Rome when he died. I remember seeing the newspaper, the headline in the late edition of *Il Messaggero*: "CAMPBELL E MORTO." Terrible.'

Pearson had been present in 1964 when Campbell achieved his ambition to be the first to break 400 mph, but the mark, set in July of that year, lasted only until the following October, when Walt Arfons sped across the Bonneville saltpan at 413.20 mph. Arfons' machine, the *Wingfoot Express*, was driven solely by the thrust from its jet engine, unconnected to its wheels—a new and more potent kind of vehicle. In another sense, however, Campbell's record lasted until October 2001, when Don Vesco of Murrieta, California used a car called *The Turbinator* at Bonneville to raise the record for cars with driven wheels to 458.44 mph. Only a few months before Vesco's run, Campbell's body was recovered from Coniston Water. It was thirty-four years since his *Bluebird* boat, travelling at close to its maximum speed, had risen from the lake's surface like a plane taking off and immediately somersaulted, breaking up as it landed on its back, and killing its driver.

'Thank our lucky stars, I suppose, that we've still got the old boat,' Campbell says at one point in Pearson's narrative, trying to keep his own spirits up as the Lake Eyre project collapses around him, threatening to destroy the meaning of his existence along with it. 'She's a bit ancient now, but she's still good for another crack at the world record!' There are many such moments here. Beautifully told, *Bluebird and the Dead Lake* is the story of an unusual kind of heroism, one helpless to avert its own fate.

I

Journey to the Lake

Adelaide in early May. The South Australian winter had almost begun. The big plane trees beside the parks were shedding their leaves, the beaches were emptying. After London it seemed a lonely, gentle, forgotten place. In the afternoons thick rain cloud would billow across the city as if a rubber factory had suddenly caught fire. It was impossible to find a taxi anywhere.

Reporters tell you May in South Australia is a bad time for news, but the papers seemed to have enough disaster and impending disaster to go round. There was to be a transport strike the following week unless someone did something about it. One of Sukarno's bombers had crashed in the Celebes with the loss of all six men on board. Another vice probe was in full swing in Sydney. And there on the back page of the *Adelaide Advertiser* for Saturday 2 May was all the latest about Campbell.

It was the sort of news appropriate for back pages of newspapers, with the big aerial photograph of a stretch of Lake Eyre under water and the car like a silhouette of dismembered aircraft fuselage, reflected forlornly in the middle of it.

It looked very dead.

'Bluebird of Unhappiness' was the headline in forty-eight point bold, for caption writers in Australia have as much liberty to state the obvious as anywhere else in the free world. The reporter had done a neat burial job on poor Donald too. There was an interview with him—very full, very fair, very sad.

'This is heart-break, Donald Campbell said today as his trial runs were again postponed.' Twenty-four points of water had fallen the night before the picture was taken and he had already flown up and down the track inspecting the damage. In places there was still an inch of water. Once again his attempt on the record had ground to a halt.

I tried thinking of Campbell and his predicament up there, four hundred miles to the north, with his car and his camp of technicians and his flooded, solitary salt lake in the middle of the great Antipodean nowhere. Record breaking is like revolution. Success is its only excuse and failure diminishes everyone in contact with it.

I knew that Campbell had staked everything on this last throw of his, but back in London the idea of staking everything on something as essentially absurd as a motor car record had seemed almost a joke. Even for him it had. I had heard him say it once or twice at parties when people asked him whether he was really going to do it this time.

'Well, I've put so much into it, old boy, that it looks as if it will have to be my neck or the record.' And he would wink at whoever had asked the question, and no one would know whether the wink was serious or not. Some people say he winks too much. He has very pale eyes, the lightest possible shade of blue. I could not imagine him winking at anyone up at Lake Eyre at the moment.

The only person I had met in Adelaide who knew him well was Florence. An old friend of the Campbells, she is tough, she is senti-mental, and she runs the best nightclub in Adelaide. When she met me off the Sydney plane she was suffering from a mild attack of laryngitis which gave all her news a curiously sepulchral quality. Only that morning she had got through by telephone to Campbell's wife, Tonia, up at the lake and learned that Campbell was planning to fly down to Adelaide on Sunday afternoon.

'Things sounded real rough,' she croaked. '*Real* rough. I just don't see how Donald can take another beating like this. They're all sitting round on the edge of that bloody silly lake, and nobody knows whether the car can run or what they can do. Tonia says he's not sleeping well. It seems like the end of the road for him, though for God's sake don't tell him I said so.'

Florence looks like a cross between Judy Garland and a swimming instructress. She wore pink satin slacks and gold slippers to meet me, and next day, although Adelaide is known as the city of churches, and although it was the Sabbath, she was wearing them again as she waited with me at the airport for Campbell's aircraft to arrive.

Adelaide has a clean, rather sleepy airport, and on Sunday afternoons it is particularly quiet, with large notices everywhere prohibiting the unauthorised transit of fruit from one state to another. Florence's laryngitis had improved, and while we waited and I grew worried about lunch, she told me about her husband and how she was flying up to Surabaya in a few days for her divorce. 'He's a Norwegian sea-captain. He's very good-looking and I'm fond of him. The only trouble is we hardly ever seem to meet. I mean, when you even have to go to a place like Indonesia to get parted from your old man, there's not much future in the marriage is there?'

Either the thought of her husband or the thought of leaving him seemed to cheer her up, and I asked her about Campbell.

'Attractive? Oh no, not attractive. Not Donald. Not in any *conventional* way.' She shook her head. 'Not to me anyhow and perhaps that's just as well, since Tonia's a great friend of mine and I've booked her to sing at a gala night at the club when he's got the record. No, he's not sexy or anything like that, but he can be very exciting. Whenever I'm near him I get the feeling that something's going to happen. Things always happen when Donald's around. That's for sure.'

It was nearly two by now and there was no sign of a plane. I asked Florence whether she thought Campbell ever could get the record.

'He could. Mind you, he's an odd man and Lake Eyre's an odd place. Once you're in a place like that anything can happen. But I think the salt will dry out for him quicker than anyone thinks. Up where the track is, near the Simpson Desert, the sun's so hot it's been known to dehydrate the body of a man completely in a few hours. Every drop of moisture dried right out of him. Dry as a bone. That's how they find the body of anyone who gets lost up round Lake Eyre.'

It was shortly after two that the afternoon Ansett plane roared down the silent runway with its load of trippers returning from Kangaroo Island, and Florence spotted Campbell's plane circling in behind it. It was blue and white and looked very small. It had a high tailfin and seemed to hop down after the Ansett plane like some busy insect that had buzzed after it all the way from Kangaroo Island. It unloaded the weekenders with their suitcases and their sunburns and their large healthy children. Then I saw Campbell.

He was walking across the tarmac with a blue leather holdall, the same small, rather jaunty man I remembered from London. He had the same raffish air, the same navy-blue blazer with the *Bluebird* buttons. He was wearing one of the shirts he has specially made for him, a particular shade of *Bluebird* blue, by a firm in Jermyn Street. Tonia walked quietly by his side.

'Well, he *looks* all right,' said Florence.

But when I went out to meet him, I saw that he had changed. His face was thinner and greyer than when I saw him last. The tendons of his neck were showing. He had had a terrible haircut.

'How are you feeling?' I asked.

'Not much use for anything really, old sport. Not much use.' He had a faint stammer I had never noticed before, and his defeat seemed total and inescapable. He had a particular look I remembered from the wartime newsreels of pilots who had been shot down and escaped with nothing but their lives.

But this was only the start. For on 3 May in the second week of his attempt on the land speed record of the world, Donald Campbell still had not driven his car.

Campbell's haggard appearance was not only due to the hammering he had had up at the lake.

On the face of it he should have been able to take a setback like this in his stride. Already he had held more world speed records than any man alive, and he had not won them easily. In one of his earliest attempts on the water speed record in 1951 on Lake Coniston, his propeller-driven *Bluebird* boat hit a submerged log at speed and had to be completely scrapped. Soon after this John Cobb had been killed on Loch Ness when his boat *Crusader* was shaken to pieces by high-frequency vibrations at a speed of around 200 mph, and the death of the imperturbable Cobb, already holder of the world land speed record of 394.4 miles an hour, seemed to show the folly of everything Campbell was attempting. People began to speak of a mysterious water barrier which would destroy any boat at these unexplored speeds.

But Campbell had gone on. With two young designers, Lewis and Ken Norris, who had just formed their own small firm of consulting engineers near Brighton, he had built a revolutionary jet-propelled hydroplane, and on 23 July 1955, at Ullswater, this new *Bluebird* broke through the water barrier which killed Cobb and set up a new water speed record of 202 miles an hour.

Nevertheless, Campbell's reputation for bad luck continued. Two months later he went to Lake Mead in Nevada to establish a new water speed record in America, and *Bluebird* sank on the first attempt. He and his team had to raise it and completely overhaul it before he could push the record up to 216 miles an hour.

This second record of his was the high spot of his career. The Foreign Office wrote congratulating him. The Queen decorated him. The Las Vegas Chamber of Commerce presented him with a vast and untarnishable gold pot which stands today in the hall of his Surrey mansion recording 'the courage and scientific achievement of Donald Campbell in raising the world speed record to 216 miles an hour on the waters of Lake Mead and so showing the possibilities of the lake as an area of aquatic recreation'.

But success at Lake Mead was also the start of the trouble which was to culminate at Lake Eyre. It was the beginning of his dream of becoming the fastest man on land as well as on water.

Possibly it was all an enormous mistake. All his experience as a record breaker had been on water, and he had never driven so much as an ordinary racing car at speed. Also it was arguable that by then the days of the big record breaking car were already over, that the motor car had got very nearly as fast as it ever would, and that in the age of astronauts few people cared whether Cobb's record stood or fell.

But if Donald Campbell's decision in 1955 to build a record-breaking car was a mistake, it was a mistake in the grandest possible manner. The car he planned was to be even more revolutionary than his boat. It would be driven through its fifty-two-inch tyres by a specially adapted aircraft gas turbine developing over five thousand brake horse-power. It would be constructed like the body of an aircraft and have mechanical brakes designed to operate at four hundred miles an hour plus. The car was stressed to withstand a total load of thirty tons on the suspension. Campbell has a touch of extravagance to his nature which reflected in his plans for the car. Typically, it was going to be the fastest, the most sophisticated, the most finely calculated car in the world.

From this moment on *Bluebird* became the centre of Campbell's life. Four more times he raised the water speed record on Lake Coniston, but building his car had become his real career and his utter obsession. His reputation depended on it. All his money was involved in it. And the way Campbell inspired and cajoled more that seventy leading British firms to contribute to it must rank as one of the most remarkable off-beat selling jobs in postwar Britain.

Campbell is rarely punctual. He lacks tact. He hates writing letters. He gets bored easily with people and has an inexplicable, almost animal capacity for arousing violent antipathy at sight in quite unlikely individuals. Yet this was a man who inspired a big oil company like BP to back him to the tune of 'something in the vicinity of a quarter of a million pounds' until the break came at the end of 1963. Dunlops built a special two-hundred-thousand-pound test plant primarily so that *Bluebird* could have the tyres it needed. (It has of course been used to test other high speed tyres since.) He got Girling to back him for his brakes, Lucas's for his electrical circuits, Smith's Industrial Instruments for his instrumentation.

The actual car, excluding its components, cost around thirty-five thousand pounds to build, but it is difficult to reach a realistic figure of how much the Bluebird Project as a whole consumed. Record bids by their very nature are expensive things to mount, especially when they take place around the other side of the world, and there was nothing cheese-paring about the scale of Campbell's operations.

Five British companies supported the record attempt with cash. Many additional companies supplied components for *Bluebird* free of cost. Some of these components were intricate and expensive—others comparatively minor, involving costs in the order of fifteen to twenty pounds.

And that afternoon in Adelaide when Campbell had flown down from Lake Eyre with disaster written all over his face every penny invested in *Bluebird* had still to pay off. His reputation, which he had staked personally to the head of each of the seventy companies, was still in the balance.

Some said it was bad luck. Others were less polite. But the fact was that *Bluebird* was still untried and Campbell had yet to prove himself and the car.

In 1960 *Bluebird* should have won the record in Utah. Instead it crashed at 360 miles an hour. Campbell suffered a broken right eardrum, a ruptured middle ear, a basal skull fracture and a contusion of the brain. But he held a press conference at his hospital in

Salt Lake City three weeks after the crash to announce that he would try again when he was better. Sir Alfred Owen, the Bible-loving Birmingham millionaire industrialist, was impressed. 'If Campbell has the guts to have another go,' he said, 'I'll build him another car.' Campbell cabled his acceptance and the idea of a second *Bluebird* was born.

This was the car lapping the water of Lake Eyre now. A large tailfin had been added to cut down the risk of a repetition of the Utah crash, but basically it was built to the same design as the original *Bluebird*.

For Campbell the 1963 record bid in Australia had been the disaster to end all disasters. He and the Bluebird Project were already on trial and everything imaginable had gone wrong. The Australian press had crucified him. The rains had come and flooded the lake. He was still suffering from the after-effects of his injuries, and when the attempt was finally called off in the middle of May, all Campbell's hopes, all those brave intentions from the days of Lake Mead had collapsed in a welter of law suits and recriminations. Stirling Moss held a special press conference to announce that in his opinion Campbell was not up to driving the car. 'He lacked,' said Moss, 'the necessary split-second reactions of a Grand Prix racing driver.'

There had been disagreements in the camp over an employee from the Owen organisation which ended with public accusations from Sir Alfred that the failure to get the record was due to mismanagement by Campbell. Campbell sued. Sir Alfred withdrew. The two men were seen shaking hands on television. 'When two gentlemen shake hands after a quarrel,' Campbell told an interviewer, 'that's the end of the matter.'

But the sour mood the whole incident left behind settled like a damp Midlands fog over the entire Bluebird Project. By 1964 no further British backers were forthcoming, and Campbell's beneficent relationship with British industry seemed almost over. BP had made any further association conditional on Campbell accepting a company nominee as manager of the

Bluebird Project and for him this was unthinkable.

So this final trip to Australia had been almost entirely at his own expense. Some of his previous supporters like Bristol Siddeley, like Girling, like Smith's Instruments and the Owen organisation had sent specialist engineers to help maintain the car when it was running. But there was no cash. The only big financial support Campbell had this time was from Ampol, an all-Australian oil company who were paying him an undisclosed sum for the right to allow *Bluebird* to run on their fuel (and more important the right to say so in the advertisements). Once the record was won this sum would be doubled and three of the English companies with components in *Bluebird* had promised substantial bonuses for their advertising rights. Without a record this time Campbell knew he could never hope to cover his costs.

But there was more than mere money at stake. There was the myth he was trying to live up to and the sort of man he was trying to be. In some ways he was the last person in the world to be expected at the centre of anything as complex and cold-blooded as modern record breaking. He had a bad medical history, with rheumatic fever as a child which caused him to be invalided out of the RAF during the war after he had been accepted for pilot training. The head injuries at Utah had added to his troubles. He is not an easy man to deal with. He is prickly. He is emotional. He is unpredictable. He is superstitious.

Above all, he is the son of his father, Sir Malcolm Campbell, and throughout his life he has had to live in the shadow of the most successful record breaker of all time.

When he died in his bed in 1948 at the age of sixty-three, Sir Malcolm Campbell had held the land speed record nine times and the water speed record three times. He had been knighted by George V after recovering the world land speed record for Britain at Daytona Beach in 1931, and he had died rich. Apart from the money made from record breaking, he had been a successful insurance broker at Lloyds, and his will revealed that he had left more than a quarter of a million.

But as well as a financial success, Sir Malcolm Campbell had been a character. Tough, lean, sharp-eyed, he was part of the fabric of the thirties. He was an amateur and a gentleman. All his success had come at a time when the world still wanted heroes like him. He had started racing at Brooklands as a sport and he had managed to keep it a sport until the end. This was a great achievement, for in these early days before speed became a branch of science fiction, he was the living proof that the machinery had not yet got out of hand. The human element still counted for something. The man was superior to the machine and he was the man.

He had first called one of his cars *Bluebird* after Maeterlinck's play, and long after the play was forgotten Campbell and *Bluebird* were still there. Already the mathematicians were taking speed to a point where it was meaningless. Already what counted was not the man in the cockpit but the scientists in the laboratories and the skill with which their missiles were launched.

But while Sir Malcolm Campbell had been inching his speeds up in battles with men like Segrave and Parry Thomas, none of this seemed to matter, and he had still been part of an older, more comprehensible tradition where sporting aristocrats drove their cars as in earlier days they drove their coaches.

Sir Malcolm Campbell was lucky in the way the thirties treated its heroes. Today fame is like one of those selective weed-killers which destroy a plant by making it grow too fast and exhausting it. Not so when he was alive. He tended his fame with careful sense and was a celebrity all his days.

But Sir Malcolm had died at the end of an era. Now at Lake Eyre Donald Campbell was still trying to continue where his father left off.

Campbell spent only one night in Adelaide. He stayed with friends on the outskirts of the city and said he slept well. Monday morning he spent shopping, buying stores needed up at the lake—a dozen extra torches, several pairs of desert boots, an anorak, blankets, a couple of bottles of embrocation—but he was anxious to get back to the lake, and we left Adelaide airport on Monday afternoon at two thirty-six South Australia time in a twin-engined Aero Commander which Campbell had chartered specially for the attempt.

There was an eight-mile-an-hour wind from the south-west, but the weather forecast was good all the way through to Alice Springs, and once we had seen the afternoon DC3 sail off behind us to Melbourne we had the sky to ourselves.

Campbell is a good pilot. He looks right in a cockpit just as he looks wrong behind a desk, and he is a surprisingly meticulous flier.

'The one place you'll never catch me fooling around is in the air,' he said as he repeated his speed and height back to the flight controller at Adelaide.

Adelaide is at the bottom of a long wedge of sea driven up towards the middle of Australia. At some time in the past the tip of the wedge connected with a chain of lakes still farther north, and Lake Eyre and Lake Torrens had both emptied into the sea. There had been forests then and heavy rainfall.

Twenty thousand years ago Lake Eyre was still part of a much larger freshwater lake called Lake Dieri. There were crocodiles at the time and large fish, and giant marsupials roamed the forests.

All this was matter now for the geologists. Slowly the river connecting the lakes with the sea had silted up and died, and with it died the whole of the flat, rich forest land around. For as the lakes lost their outlet and the waters went on evaporating, their salinity increased. The fish and the crocodiles vanished. The forests fell. The great marsupials died. And as the rainfall diminished, the whole area withered into the hot, dry desert that was our destination.

Although it continued to drain the water from a quarter of Australia, Lake Eyre died too. With each century that passed, the evaporation of the rivers flowing into it built up the layers of its salt, the salt on which Campbell was hoping to win his record.

It was a long flight, taking nearly the entire afternoon, and from six thousand feet the whole prehistory of this strange country lay stretched below. We passed Port Pirie where the railhead touches the coast and they bring the freshly mined iron ore and ship it down to Adelaide. The long purple scar of the Flinders Ranges was on the right, and ahead lay the mauve and brown emptiness of Australia's desert heart.

It was at four-twenty that we saw the first pale glint on the horizon like the sun striking a thin strip of steel, and Campbell pointed and shouted, 'There! There she is. There's the lake. We'll fly over, we've just time before dusk.'

The sun was almost down before we were there and the lake looked as flat and dead as a sheet of asbestos.

'We'll go down,' shouted Campbell above the racket of the motors. 'See how the surface is since we left.' And as the engines whined and the vertigo caught us and we spiralled our way down to within a few hundred feet of the surface, layer upon layer of colour began to appear, greens and yellows, silvers and pinks and browns, until it was like descending into the heart of a freshly opened oyster.

Campbell was enjoying himself. He was grinning now and shouting with excitement as he pulled the aircraft out of its turn and pointed down to where a narrow black speck lay like a match-stick on the strange surface of the lake.

'That's the car. That's *Bluebird*. She's still there.' And we came in lower still until we could see the outline of the steel ribs under the green canvas of the hangar where the car was housed and the guy-ropes of the tents where the mechanics kept the spares.

There were a couple of lorries and a pile of oil drums and a thin, silver-latticed radio mast. But there was no sign of life. The camp looked derelict. It could have been there for years like the headquarters of an expedition that lost it's way.

Due north ran a narrow line, as straight and precise as if ruled in pink crayon across the salt, and twice we flew over it.

'That's the track,' said Campbell. 'Fifteen miles of it. Six months to prepare. Five hundred quid a mile in preparation costs. That's where we run, when we run.'

His wife asked him what he thought of the surface of the salt. 'Not bad, not bad at all. It's certainly dried out a lot in a couple of days. The wind shifts it, you know. Actually blows the water from one side of the lake to the other, and it looks as though we might have been lucky.'

He pointed far over to the eastern shore where there was a dark blotch along the whole edge of the salt like the mark hot milk leaves on a carpet when it spills.

'That's last Friday's twenty-four points of rain. Let's just hope it evaporates before the wind changes its mind and blows it back into the centre of the track.'

The flight across the lake had put us behind schedule, and Campbell began to worry about the dark, for the airstrip had no flare-path. Muloorina, the sheep station where Campbell and all the main party were living, was thirty-five miles away, and he seemed to think we would be only just in time.

Nightfall in the outback is swift and spectacular, and the first stars were already out. The land was blurred with shadows as the wheels rasped down on the landing-strip and the propellers reversed with a whirring of air and the motor surged for the last time and was still.

'Muloorina,' said Campbell. 'We've arrived.'

I had no idea what I was stepping into as I left the aircraft. Suddenly after the roar of the motors the silence was intense. There was gravel underfoot and a great cloud of dust from the landing was beginning to settle. Two boys were there to watch us as we pulled our bags from the luggage compartment. They rode off on old bicycles without a word. A wind-pump was slowly turning at the end of the landing-strip, and beyond was a long corrugated-iron roof, silhouetted against the glow of the sunset.

We walked towards it. The silence was complete, and in the dusk the smell of the outback was on the wind, an old smell— dry, dusty, faintly aromatic. Then people came out to meet us, but they were indistinct in that half-light.

'Hi Don—Welcome back, Skipper—What're the girls like now in civilisation?'

After the noise of the aircraft the voices sounded strange in the darkness and emptiness.

'Not a bad trip, Unc,' I heard Campbell say. 'I got you a few tins of that Dunhill mixture. How's the bloody lake?'

'So-so, Skipper. So-so.'

Even this close it was too dark to distinguish faces clearly, and all I could see of the man Campbell was talking to was a short stocky figure and an old trilby hat with the brim turned down. Campbell put his arm round the man's shoulder as they walked towards one of the bungalows beyond. There was a big yard with a row of sheds on the other side. The lights were on and someone was slaughtering a sheep. The hind legs were tied to a beam and there was no noise as it had its throat cut.

2

The King of Muloorina

'Hallo, Elliot. Elliot, you old devil. Where are you? We've a new arrival. Is there a bed for him on the verandah or does he have to sleep with the girls?'

Campbell let the fly-proof door of the bungalow slam behind him, and the yellow moths that clung to it fluttered up against the light. An old dog with a ginger tail woke to see what all the fuss was about.

'Steady now, Donald. Steady,' said a voice from a door on the other side of the verandah. 'I'm not so young as I used to be, and with all your blokes here I've had a busy day of it.'

'So that's where you're hiding,' said Campbell, and still laden with his haversack and his embrocation and his tins of Dunhill's smoking mixture, he led the way into a long, brightly-lit sitting room with a blue and pink flowered carpet on the floor, a player piano against the far wall and vases of plastic lilac on the mantel-piece. Resplendent in a big green armchair was the man Campbell was looking for.

He was short and very solid with thick grey hair and mahogany-coloured arms. He wore wide, red-striped braces and a precise moustache which gave his weatherbeaten face a touch of quite extraordinary wickedness.

'This,' said Campbell, 'is the king. Elliot Price, King of Muloorina.'

'That's right,' he said. 'Except for the lake. That's not in my territory. In the state it's in now, I'll let you be king of Lake Eyre, Donald.'

'How is the course?' asked Campbell quickly. 'When we flew over it just now it didn't look too bad.'

'Well, Donald, I've been here twenty-one years and I still don't understand that bloody lake. Last year before you came it had a surface like concrete. Then you had your rain. Soon as you arrived if you remember.'

'Yes,' said Campbell grimly, 'I remember.'

'First rain it had had for eight years. Now it starts again, soon as you turn up, for the second year running. I don't understand these things, Donald, and I can't say I want to. All I do know is that when I first came here the blacks would never have anything to do with the lake. Wouldn't go near the place. And the blackfellows have their reasons for these things. So you can have it, Donald. I'll stick to my sheep. Sheep's chancy things, but I still prefer them.'

'Well, if I do as well out of the lake as you've done out of your sheep, Elliot, I shan't do too badly.'

'P'raps, Donald,' said the old man, smiling to himself and shaking his head. 'We'll see.'

'What d'you mean, we'll see?' said Campbell, suddenly anxious to change the subject. 'How much are you worth, Elliot? Let's have the truth. Have you made your million yet?'

'Now, Donald,' said the old man, yawning and scratching his chest, 'that'd be telling, and to be truthful I'm not sure of the answer myself. We've enough to be comfortable. I've got the plane and the new Buick for myself. I run twelve thousand sheep and all the money goes back into the business. There's fourteen mile of inch-and-a-quarter plastic piping for me waiting to be collected in the goods yard at Marree at the moment. Fourteen mile at two bob a foot, work it out for yourself. That's where the money goes.'

And this was where much of Elliot Price's money had been going from the day towards the end of 1942 when he arrived at Muloorina with a thousand pounds and an old Dennis truck. He was forty-one and had made his living until then as a travelling well-borer. It was because he reckoned he could find water near Muloorina that he had gambled all his savings and settled his family on this forgotten strip of desert bordering the southern shores of Lake Eyre.

When he came he had found a deserted homestead dating back to the days when this part of Australia had been used to breed the camels whose ancestors had been imported from Afghanistan for the great journeys of exploration across Australia in the 1870s. For years the camel trails had passed this way, north-east along the Birdsville Track, skirting the parched desert lands towards Alice Springs and beyond.

Then the lorries had taken over, and in batches of forty and fifty at a time the camels, like obsolescent machines, had been brought to Muloorina to be destroyed. So when Elliot Price arrived at Muloorina he found great piles of camel bones around the homestead. Being an economical man he had used them to mark out his airstrip.

This common sense was typical of him and the way he took this dead land and put it to his own uses. He drilled for water, and with the thirteenth shaft he found it as he said he would. He also discovered the tough, water-bearing roots and the lichens and succulents that could keep sheep alive on land that might go without rain for five years in succession. And he and his children and their children in their turn had built Muloorina into a family kingdom over which Elliot Price ruled like the head of some feudal dynasty.

It was a kingdom he had kept jealously within his family. Each of his married children had a bungalow within walking distance of the main homestead building, and in his cellars Elliot Price kept sufficient stores to last the whole community six months. The South Australian government supplied a teacher who ran a school in which every pupil was a Price grandchild.

'You know what I've been doing today, Donald?' said the old man as he got up to go into supper. 'Been choosing a spot for my grave. Finally settled on that bit of rising ground beside the track from Marree where you first catch sight of the homestead. When you get to my age you worry about these things. I want a big stone there so in years to come, when they've built a proper road out here, people will stop and ask what the bloody great stone's for, and someone'll say, "that's where they buried the old bastard who started it all!"'

He buttoned the neck of his shirt and began pulling an ancient grey jacket over his bull-like shoulders.

'I know it's bloody silly, but these things come to matter, Donald. They matter a lot.'

'I know they do, Elliot,' replied Campbell softly, 'I know.'

Perhaps it was the influence of Elliot Price that produced the distinctly feudal air all the meals at Muloorina seemed to share. The men sat together at a long table, with Price enthroned at one end in a large wooden armchair. Campbell, in a slightly smaller one, sat at the other.

This male, tribal world seemed to suit Campbell. His face lost its lines and the greyness of Adelaide. Now that he was back among people he knew and trusted, the record bid was no longer the ordeal of a lonely man. It was what it always should have been—an adventure to be shared, and the more people who joined in the better.

It was interesting to watch him at dinner that first evening. Leo Villa, Campbell's chief engineer, was on his left, a solid, avuncular presence in a khaki shirt. He was the man wearing the trilby hat who had been waiting for us that night on the landing-strip, and he was an important part of the whole Campbell legend. For Leo Villa was not merely Campbell's engineer—he was his friend, his conscience, and his most important link with the past. If Campbell was Quixote, Villa was Sancho Panza. He had joined

Sir Malcolm Campbell as mechanic when he was twenty-three, and had been with the family ever since. Campbell still called him 'Unc'. He had built the *Bluebird* car of 1935—the first car to reach 300 mph—with his own hands, and he had more first-hand experience of record breaking than any man alive. He is the sort of man who never changes, and it was inevitable that when Sir Malcolm died he should have carried on his life's work with the son.

Opposite Villa sat Ken Norris, the third key man in the *Bluebird* team. He held a degree in aeronautical engineering from Imperial College, London, and his brother Lewis had designed both the car and the record breaking *Bluebird* jet boat. At one time his company had twenty people working on the designs for the car, and put in a total of 36,000 design hours. A slim, determined man, whose nose was already peeling from the harsh sun of the outback, he ate less than either Campbell or Villa and had a habit of answering direct technical questions by working out impromptu sums on stamp-sized pieces of paper. But he needed no calculations to answer the one question Campbell slipped in quite casually while the soup was still on the table.

'Is the car ready?'

'Had a look at her this morning. As far as we could see she was fine.'

'And how was the salt?'

'Well, that's more difficult to be precise about.' He pushed his hair back across his forehead and looked at Campbell, smiling a faint non-committal smile which could have meant anything. 'Ask Leo. He's the salt expert.'

'Always hard to say on this bloody lake,' said Villa. The soup was very good and he was halfway through his second plateful. He enjoys his food, and the sunburned dome of his head gleamed benevolently above his spectacles. 'The water's gone from the surface for the first few miles of the track, but I wouldn't like to say how hard the salt is, Skipper. And I wouldn't like to give my guarantee for the middle of that track of yours. I know Andrew

Mustard has put a hell of a lot of work into it, but I've always had my doubts.'

'You have, have you, Unc?' said Campbell. 'Where is Andrew, incidentally?'

'Still down in Adelaide. Should be back tomorrow or the day after that.'

'Ah,' said Campbell.

Now that he was here everyone seemed to have come alive, for he has an undeniable way with him, the same quality his father is said to have had, of entering a room and making himself the focus of everyone's attention.

'I don't know what you and your boys are thinking of doing with yourselves while the lake dries out,' said Price suddenly. 'But I'm planning to go up towards Cooper's Creek, baiting for dingoes. If you and any of the boys'd like to come along for the ride, Donald, you'd all be more'n welcome.'

'Dingo baiting?' said someone. 'How d'you do that, Elliot?'

'You poisons the buggers. Strychnine in kangaroo meat. You puts it down the burrows.'

'But why poison them? Why not shoot them?' said Campbell.

'Takes too long and they're too bloody hard to hit. You ever tried hitting a dingo, Don? Christ, they're smart are dingoes. And beautiful. The most beautiful bastard creature you could hope to see, a well fed dingo. And intelligent. The stories I could tell you about dingoes. But them's the biggest foul killers in the country. They'll tear the guts out of a couple of dozen sheep, one after the other, just for the fun of it.'

The old man paused, elbows on table, to take a good mouthful of his own mutton.

'That's why you poisons 'em. So's I say, Donald, if you or your boys feel like a day or two up by the Cooper, you're more'n welcome. It's interesting country up there. You heard of Burke an' Wills the explorers—it's right near where they copped it.'

'Well, it's kind of you, Elliot, old sport, but I think we'll all be having work to do tomorrow.'

As Campbell said this, I saw Leo Villa look up sharply and for a moment it seemed as if he would speak. But he kept quiet and Campbell went on.

'One thing I wanted to ask you, Elliot. Earlier this evening you were talking about the lake and the way the Aborigines would never go near it. What did you mean?'

'Oh, nothing, Don. They have these funny ideas of theirs. Forget it.'

'But damn it, Elliot. This is your country. Just tell me about this lake. You know what happened last year as well as I do. It hadn't rained there for eight years. Then the night the army finished building the causeway for us, what happened? The heavens opened. Fine, we said, it's an exception, a freak. The lake dried out and we got ready to run on May the eighth. And the night of May the seventh what happened again? Once more the heavens opened, and we were washed out. Now this year, Elliot, everyone told us there couldn't possibly be rain two years running. The chances of it happening were God knows how many hundred to one. And yet we come, we get ready to run, and then last Friday night the same thing happens. So what about that?'

Price seemed in two minds over what to reply.

'Well, you know how it is, Don. The abo can understand things we can't. They say he can make rain and cause drought. He can put the finger on someone and two days later he's dead. No one knows how. There's no mark on the body. He's just dead. Well,' and he paused to belch before continuing, 'the lake has always been considered a place of death by the abo. He won't go on it and he's always warned the white man not to. It's a sort of legend here. But you don't want to take any notice of that sort of silly nonsense. Superstition's all right for these ignorant simple buggers, but of course there's nothing in it. We've all been on the lake, haven't we—yet we're still here.'

Leo Villa had a box of fifty small Manila cheroots and there was silence as he passed them round the table. All Campbell's attention seemed to be concentrated on his cigar. He moistened the end, snipped it deftly with a small steel cutter, and waited until the match he was holding to the end had nearly burned to his fingers before drawing his first puff.

'Unc, how long did Andrew Mustard say he would be staying down in Adelaide?'

'Till Wednesday, Skipper. He said in the state the lake's in at the moment it would be impossible to have a run before then.'

'He did, did he. Well that's a pity, because I think we're going to have a go tomorrow morning.'

The promise of action was the most precious gift Campbell had to offer, and that evening I had the first taste of the weird excitement which was to build up and then vanish so many times in the weeks ahead.

Remember the isolation of the place, the silence of the nights and the slowness with which day was to succeed day. Remember the loneliness and the feeling the outback can give that you are becalmed, helpless in an ocean of desert. With all this, the promise of each new run with the car was to turn into the one drug which could make this place tolerable.

But that first night the excitement was still real, and incidents stick in the memory in a way they never did afterwards. There was Leo Villa taking Campbell into the kitchen and sitting him down with a cup of tea at the long table covered with green and white checked American cloth, and telling him how dangerous the rain-softened salt was still likely to be.

When Villa gets excited his spectacles mist up, and he talks very fast as if he is back in the pits of Brooklands snatching a few seconds before his driver slams in the clutch and roars off again around the track.

'But Don, listen. It's crazy trying anything on that track tomorrow. We don't know what it's like. Anything could happen on it. We just don't know.'

The situation was clearly one Campbell had been facing with

Leo Villa on and off through most of his life, and he was very calm, very reasonable with him. He put a lot of sugar in his tea and waited for the old man to finish.

'Well, Unc,' he said, 'if we don't know we've just got to find out, haven't we?' And he smiled his most reassuring smile and put his hand on his shoulder and winked, and Leo Villa knew, from long experience, that there was nothing else to be said.

Later there was a briefing in one of the corrugated-iron sheds used by the sheep shearers. Everyone remotely connected with the record bid was there, crammed into that bare uncomfortable room with its scuffed concrete floor, its pile of mattresses in the corner, and its single light bulb shaded with the cover of a five-year-old copy of *Time* magazine.

There was Cliff Brebner, the gaunt, amiable superintendent from the South Australian police, who was responsible for security and communications with the lake. There was Tom Scrimshire, a large florid man, son of a Coventry butcher, who had been foreman in charge of building the car at Motor Panels. There were the technical experts—Carl Noble from Electro-Hydraulics, a former Fleet Air Arm pilot—Ken Reaks from Smith's Industrial Instruments, another former pilot—George Hammond from Bristol-Siddeleys who was responsible for *Bluebird*'s Proteus turbine, and Tom Lawson and Ron Willies of Girling who had helped develop the car's brakes.

All of them were personally involved in the car's failure or success. Each of them knew that his reputation and the reputation of his firm would suffer badly if anything went wrong at speed which could later be traced to his particular components.

And as well as the technical experts, there were the drivers and men who had been working on the track. Their faces, tanned and roughened by nearly a whole summer labouring up on the lake, made the white faces of the engineers appear delicate, almost feminine by contrast. And even then, that first night, there seemed something sceptical, unimpressed about the way they listened as Campbell, another of Leo Villa's cigars between his lips, outlined the plans for the next morning's run.

'It will be in the nature of a test, gentlemen. A test for the car and a test for me. But primarily a test for the track. Frankly, no one knows how much damage last Friday's rain has done, and the only way to find out is to do what I intend to do tomorrow morning.'

On occasions such as these Campbell is at his best—crisply articulate, very sure of himself, like an actor who has really learned his lines and is beginning to enjoy his part. He was wearing a blue, battle-dress type jacket with the red, white and blue badge of the Ampol oil company on his left breast pocket.

The only questions that evening came from the one member of the Australian press to arrive so far. His name was Parr, Wally Parr, of Australian Associated Press. He had a large, brown notebook and was wearing denim overalls. He had the air of a man who was expecting trouble of one sort or another. He asked serious, factual questions, and had clearly been through the cuttings before he arrived.

'How much power will you be using, Donald?'

'That depends on what Ken Norris advises once he has seen the conditions. Probably thirty per cent of maximum.'

'That could take you up to what speed?'

'Around 280 to 300.'

'And there is no significance in the absence of Andrew Mustard?'

'No, Wally old boy. Andrew decided to have a day or two with his family down in Adelaide and will be back tomorrow or the day after.'

But the most memorable face of all that night before the first run was not at the meeting in the shearers' quarters. It was at the homestead, and it belonged to Campbell's wife, Tonia.

She was in the sitting room alone. It was just after eleven, and the Prices and the rest of the family were asleep already. In the dining room, beyond the swing doors with the frosted glass, her husband was discussing the car's probable performance with its chief designer. Sheets of graph paper were scattered across the brown felt table cover. Norris had his slide-rule, Campbell his pipe, and although the doors were closed the low buzz of their voices could be heard from where she was sitting.

But she took no notice. All her attention was on her embroidery—a small needlework picture of a South Sea island—and she worked deftly, methodically, a determined woman, used to taking trouble to get what she wanted. She is Flemish. Her father owns a large hotel near Ostend. She is tall and has the sort of good looks that make mere prettiness somehow irrelevant. That evening she had taken charge of the kitchen and done most of the cooking. Soup was her speciality.

Slowly the leaves of a small palm tree took shape from her needle.

'You're not seeing the real man here at all, you know,' she said, nodding in the direction of the dining room. 'These last few months have been hell for all of us, him particularly.'

She went on sewing, and the buzz of conversation from the dining room continued.

'I wish to God he wouldn't do it. I admire him for it. Tremendously. I admire people who won't give in. But I wish it was all happening to somebody else's husband. You see, this is his life. Everything he stands for and believes in is at stake in this thing.

'He's a strange man you know,' she went on. 'He's very brave and very superstitious and very tender. And if you want to understand him you really have to begin with his father.'

She stopped sewing, and pulled her thick pink angora sweater around her for the room was suddenly cold. The gold slippers she wore made a discreet protest against the overstuffed green armchairs and brown bulk of the piano.

'Was the soup all right tonight?' she said. 'The trouble with this place is the onions. Have you seen a good onion since you've been in Australia?'

3
The Lizards

There is a small, extremely rare albino lizard, about four inches long with pink eyes and a furtive manner. It is not an attractive animal. Until it moves it looks as if it has been pressed from white polythene. When startled its tail drops off.

But this lizard is unique. It has succeeded where men and all other animals have failed. It has learned to live on the surface of Lake Eyre, feeding, as far as one can discover, on flies and small insects which get blown on to the salt.

Normally you never see it, even after months on the lake, for apart for its rarity, its grubby white skin blends in perfectly with the grubby white surface of the salt. Why, during the course of its evolution, it should have bothered to camouflage itself in this way, must remain one of the minor puzzles of zoology. For this lizard has no known competitors in its battle for existence. Until Campbell arrived it was the only thing to have found a use for this four thousand miles of salty nothingness.

At various times, it is true, the lizards are challenged in their possession of the lake, but not for long. Occasionally rabbits appear from nowhere and flock on to it, struggling over the soft mud that lines the shores like a treacherous brown moat. Duck and parrots have been found there. Fat brown grasshoppers are sometimes blown on to it in their thousands by the great, dust-bearing winds that come sweeping across from the desert.

Men have tried to challenge the lizards too. In the 1840s and 1850s, after Edward John Eyre first viewed the lake and gave it his name, Lake Eyre became one of the great Australian mysteries which later explorers set themselves to solve. One of them reported cliffs and fresh water there. Another insisted these were the effect of mirages. Another said it was surrounded by meadows of rich grass.

It was not until the end of the century that the truth about Lake Eyre began to be known and the geologists discovered how this immense, normally dry salt bed was the focus of a great internal drainage system for half a million square miles of central Australia.

But even then there was no certainty about the place. Were there minerals there to be mined? Was there oil? No one knew. The explorers were succeeded by aerial surveys, and the aerial surveys by the drilling rigs of the Department of Mines. It was estimated that the lake contained four hundred million tons of salt and that its surface varied between 39 and 29.2 feet below sea level. Investigation showed that in places the salt crust was up to fifteen inches thick. Beneath that was mud—thick black primeval mud— and as the trial drills of the geologists probed downwards through it they brought up mineral specimens of exuberant variety. There was gypsum and mica, palygorskite and montmorillonite. Kaolin and geothite appeared at a depth of 145 feet and alunite between 153 and 156 feet.

It was all very interesting but it was not what the Department of Mines was looking for. The drilling rigs departed and the lizards once again were left in peace.

It was in 1961 that Campbell came for the first time. After his car had crashed on the salt flats at Utah he had decided that for his next record bid he would have to find somewhere else— somewhere longer, smoother, flatter and less crowded. For at Utah in 1960 the track had been a mere ten and a half miles; the surface had been made treacherous by the oil from other cars, and he had been under the constant pressure of having speed trials going on throughout the time he was there.

Any of these factors could have contributed to the crash. And none of them was likely to worry him on Lake Eyre.

He had heard about Lake Eyre through British Petroleum who were still retaining him in those days, and in the spring he had flown out from Britain specially to see this mysterious lake which nobody had beard about and only the largest atlases bothered to record. It had been a nightmare journey for him. He was still suffering the after-effects of the crash, and in San Francisco he had had a nervous attack so severe that he nearly called off the entire visit. Instead he took sleeping pills, and the Qantas manager at the airport arranged for him to travel the rest of the way in the crew bunk.

BP met him at the airport at Adelaide. By then the attack was over. Campbell borrowed a hat with a wide brim and flew to Muloorina the following day. As soon as he saw the lake he knew he had found what he wanted. 'I could hardly believe it,' he says. 'The surface was like concrete. It was flat, it was smooth and it seemed to go on for ever.'

He had flown up with several companions. One was a Dutchman called Dolph Lengton who worked for BP as an area manager and had suggested Lake Eyre in the first place. Another was a thin man with a red beard who worked for Dunlops and had been at Utah when *Bluebird* crashed. His name was Andrew Mustard. And at Muloorina Campbell met Elliot Price for the first time and Blue Hughes, Elliot's son-in-law.

Campbell's party stayed at Muloorina several days. Hughes knew a spot where it was possible to cross the mud and get on to the surface of the lake, so that surveys were done on foot as well as from the air. Campbell wore his wide-brimmed hat and carried a long tool called an auger to measure the thickness of the salt. He compared the salt of Lake Eyre with the salt he remembered from Utah and was very happy. By the time he was ready to fly back to Adelaide a large slice of his future had already been decided.

There were difficulties of course. The lake was inaccessible—thirty-eight miles of spring-breaking bush track to Muloorina and another forty miles to the railhead at Marree after which there were three changes of gauge along the track to Adelaide. A solid causeway would have to be built across the mud to the hard salt of the lake. And a fifteen-mile track, fifty yards wide, would need to be marked out and smoothed, free of blemishes, flat as a billiard table, somewhere on the lake. At Utah this had been done by pulling heavy drags made of railway lines across the salt. It was a slow business, but there seemed no reason why it should not work here as well.

During his fourteen years as a record breaker, Campbell had grown used to overcoming difficulties.

When he saw Sir Thomas Playford, the veteran Premier of South Australia, he had found things easier than he hoped. The two men got on well together. Once again, as so many times in the past, Campbell described the adventure, the excitement of what he was trying to do, an adventure in which South Australia had a chance to share. If it succeeded—and provided the Bluebird Project received its necessary assistance, there was no reason why it should not succeed—Lake Eyre could replace Bonneville and Daytona as the new centre of international record breaking.

That November, Campbell gave back the wide-brimmed hat to its owner and returned to London a happy man. Everything, it seemed, was arranged. The South Australian government promised to build a causeway on to the lake and improve the road from Muloorina. The Australian federal government said they would lend troops when the record bid began. And Campbell was granted a lease on the lake for one pound (Australian) a year payable in advance. The lizards had found themselves a new competitor.

'It depends on the lake,' Campbell was saying. 'If there's a chance in hell of getting her rolling today, darling, I've got to take it.

Everyone's been hanging around doing nothing far too long. Morale will simply go if we don't get moving.'

It was six-fifteen in the morning and Campbell was walking to the airstrip with his wife, still carrying the blue holdall he had with him on arrival at Adelaide. Early as it was, dawn was almost over. The greens and mauves and magentas of sunrise were slipping from the horizon, but the air was still sharp and a last star flickered in the west.

'But you never do get ideal conditions. You must just grab what you can while it's there to be grabbed.' Campbell's voice echoed back across the flat stillness of the morning, a melancholy statement of fact. Tonia said nothing in reply.

There was nothing she could say. She wore a pink and white scarf around her hair and had a heavy shrouded look. Three black crows loped across the sky as they reached the aircraft.

Peter Ahrens, the senior pilot from the aircraft hire firm, was already waiting in the cockpit, but it seemed taken for granted that Campbell was to handle the controls. Ahrens is a solid, scrupulous man with short blond hair and a thick Swedish neck. He is twenty-eight and his uniform shirts are very white. Campbell went through the aircraft's check list very carefully.

'Flaps. Up and checked.'

'Trim tabs. Set and checked.'

'Seat belts. Secure.'

His voice was emphatic, measured—a good actor's voice. I noticed a scar on his right ear. A dog bit him there when he was eight and it was badly cut again in the Utah crash.

The port engine coughed, then spluttered into life. The starboard followed. He synchronised them, opened the throttle twice with the brakes still on, set his compass, and we taxied across the drumming red surface of the airstrip between the mangy dogs and the silent children on old bicycles, past the carcasses of the abandoned lorries, the thickets of rusting beer cans, broken glass, mouldering farm implements. Then, gathering speed, we chased the barbed-wire fence towards the wind sock and took off with the sun already risen away on our right in the wide yellow sky.

Tonia was sitting directly behind her husband. She looked as if she had not slept well, and put on her sunglasses when the sun came glittering into the cabin.

Campbell flew with great assurance, taking the Commander up in a wide sweep away from Muloorina, until we were heading north-east for the lake. It was a worn, leather-coloured landscape we were flying over—an endless overwhelming land.

For a while we followed the Frome, most despairing of rivers, as it faltered across that parched country, splitting, twisting, almost disappearing on its hopeless journey towards the salt lake. Farther north the line of a dingo fence threaded across the wilderness before it too disappeared. Then the lake came into view, and as we drew towards it we could see layer upon layer of colour swirling off into the distance as the sunlight struck the surface of the salt.

We came in lower, passing the edge of the lake at a few hundred feet, just above the wide rim of mud separating the salt from the land.

To the left, a neat brown line, at right angles to the shore, was the causeway. It was over half a mile long, constructed of rock and earth. Aircraft apart, everything entering or leaving the lake had to cross it.

We circled the camp once. Campbell pointed down to the fresh trucks and cars clustered around the tank shelter where *Bluebird* was housed.

'Looks as if we're expected,' he said, and glanced back, smiling at Tonia. Even that brief spell at the controls of the Commander had done him good. He appeared more assured, more confident than I had seen him and suddenly determined to prove that today was his day and that he and no one else was in command.

'Fine,' she said, and took off the sunglasses to smile at him. She has a very beautiful smile—wide, confident, holding nothing back. 'It'll be just fine today, darling.'

And as if to prove her right Campbell made a perfect landing with the wheels producing only the faintest crackling on the salt as we touched down, the sort of noise a cycle makes across snow which has turned to slush and then frozen again.

Leo Villa and his two mechanics had been on the lake since five, preparing the car, and as we climbed from the aircraft the old man came out to meet us, a solid, rather bandy figure with his large, green-lensed spectacles and his oil-stained canvas hat.

'What's it like, Unc?'

'Well, the car's ready when you are, Skipper. Has been for weeks. It's not the car I'm worried about, it's this bloody salt.' And he stamped with his heel on the salt and pointed to the soft imprint it left behind.

'That's your trouble, Skipper. No guts in it. You can kick a hole in it if you want to. The water from the other night hasn't evaporated as we hoped. It's soaked in and whole lake's one big bloody sponge.'

Villa shares Campbell's habit of overdramatising things and often repeats his best phrases for effect.

'Just like a bloody sponge, Skipper,' and as he spoke he stamped again on the salt.

Behind him was the camp. The tank shelter was bigger than it had looked from the air—it could almost have housed a small airship—and round it was all the paraphernalia of a record attempt—oil drums, lengths of piping, a small generating plant and battered wooden packing cases with 'Campbell—Bluebird—Adelaide' stencilled in large black letters on the side.

There was a mobile army workshop, a water trailer, a pair of bright yellow Toyota fuelling trucks from Ampol, and several lorries and cars. But despite all these signs of activity the whole camp had an air of isolation to it. The sun was beginning to build up its power by now and glared down on the weird landscape of the lake with a brilliance that cut us off completely from any world beyond. Despite the heat there was something Arctic about it all.

The light was clear and intense and cruel. Once out in it away from the camp a man would be swallowed up as certainly as if he lost his way at the North Pole. An individual here would count for very little. Brightness, silence, solitude—this was Lake Eyre. Beyond the camp there was nothing, no landmark, no sign of life—only the bright even circle of the horizon and the glaring sun and the sky above the palest blue.

It was a silent wilderness. There were no birds to cry, no animals to call. The only sound was the faint whimpering of the wind in the radio mast and the crunch of our own feet as we walked across to the car.

'Well, what d'you think of her?' said Campbell, slapping *Bluebird* as a farmer might slap the flank of a dearly-bought heifer.

Inside the dim, green, creosote-smelling cavern of *Bluebird*'s canvas hangar, it was difficult to know what to think. The wheel fairings were off the car, and the mechanics were checking the wheels. By the light of the inspection lamps *Bluebird* looked incomplete, threatening, a thing of mystery. It was far bigger than the photographs made it appear. It was also more frightening. Watching the mechanics working on it was like watching the final preparations on some space rocket—the long, carefully polished blue body, the great snout with the air intake at the front, and the tailfin with the glaucous eye of the automatic camera let into the leading edge.

This was the end of the line, the motor car which is driven through its wheels developed to its ultimate, and become so specialised that all it could be used for was one lonely task—to flash across a carefully prepared mile of salt in the middle of Australia faster than any car had gone before.

The existing record of 394 mph had been set by John Cobb in 1948. Since then Craig Breedlove had reached 412 mph in a jet-propelled car with three wheels. But Breedlove's speed had not been a world record. At that time the Fédération Internationale d'Automobile in Paris was still refusing to recognise jet-propelled vehicles for the speed record. Only a car like *Bluebird*, driven through the wheels, was eligible.

Villa and his two assistants had been in Australia since February working on the car—cleaning it, stripping it down, polishing it, rebuilding it. After the washout of the previous year it had been stored in a repository in Adelaide.

'It's a brand-new motor car,' said Leo Villa. 'Practically unused. Never been run on anything like full power. Used for only a few runs last year and then packed away.'

Campbell did not stay long inside the tank shelter looking at his car. Now that he had seen the salt for himself, Villa's doubts about the wisdom of making a run seemed to be worrying him too. A group of technicians had gathered outside the hangar waiting for something to happen. Norris was among them.

'Ken, what d'you think of the surface?' asked Campbell.

'Not much, but the water's certainly disappeared quicker than I thought it would. The question is where it's gone to.' His voice trailed off. He is a diffident man and dislikes getting into a position where he has to give advice publicly.

Campbell turned away, stamped once or twice on the salt as Villa had done and looked carefully at the imprint of his boot as if it held the answer to all his problems.

'Okay, Unc,' he called across to Villa at the entrance to the hangar. 'You say she's ready. Let's have her out and take a look at her.'

It was seven-fifteen. A dozen pairs of hands helped slide the car out. She came slowly, like a big animal from a lair. The sun gleamed on her.

Apart from the faintest of nods to Tonia, Campbell never actually announced his decision to make that first run in *Bluebird*, but once the car had been brought out it was as if we had no choice. She had to run. And everyone took it for granted now that she would.

Campbell stood for a while talking to Villa. Then the yellow fuelling truck was brought up to pump the fourteen gallons for the run into *Bluebird*'s tank. The booster vehicle with the generator to start the turbine followed.

For Campbell the start of each run demanded an elaborate ritual. This was where the blue holdall came in. It held the regalia of the record breaker—the objects without which he would never have dreamt of entering the cockpit. There was the oxygen mask, the blue linen helmet with the headphones for the radio, and the silver jet pilot's crash helmet which was given to him when he was getting ready for his first attempt with the *Bluebird* hydroplane by his friend Neville Duke the test pilot. There were a pair of old blue tennis shoes which he wore in the cockpit, and his two mascots Whoppit and Whacko. Whoppit, a small bear with a red coat, wore a St Christopher medal around his neck and had survived the Utah crash with his owner. An indomitable bear, he still travelled in the cockpit. The other bear, Whacko, was like the rest of us, an onlooker. Despite the name, Whacko was a lady, and after every run she had to be reunited with the fearless Whoppit.

The contents of the blue holdall were Tonia's responsibility. By long practice she knew when they were required. She knew when to hand Campbell the tennis shoes, and when to give him the silver helmet. It was done in silence. It reminded one of *Ivanhoe* or the *Romance of the Rose*. Whoppit went in last.

There was a final check through with Ken Norris leaning across the cockpit and Campbell testing brakes, and radio and controls. Then the cockpit cover was lowered over him, and all you could see was the dim outline of his face with the breathing mask and the silver crown of the crash helmet as he peered out through his one small window. Already he seemed a very long way away.

This was not like motor car racing, when there are other cars to compete against and excitement to take the driver's mind off the risks he is taking. This was a cold-blooded, lonely business. All that this driver had to compete against was his own weakness and his own fear.

A horn sounded on the booster truck. This was Campbell's own signal to start the turbine. There was a faint pause—then a thin whirring like a high-speed dentist's drill as the compressor turned within the engine. Then came the full roar as the engine came to life. A haze of brown smoke appeared. Heat flickered from the four big exhaust pipes at the tail, and *Bluebird* was ready to run for the first of her trials.

Several of us had a car ready and drove on ahead to watch *Bluebird* as she passed. We went parallel with the track and were doing over ninety when the car caught us up. Campbell was handling her gently, and the long blue car passed us with a stately, effortless gliding across the gleaming salt. It could have been flying instead of running on four wheels, and we watched as it went on ahead, picking up speed now, knifing its way up the course, past the big yellow Dunlop flag at the three-mile mark, until it nearly vanished in the glare of the horizon, the tiniest of dots floating on the mirage with a cloud of cream-coloured salt trailing like a comet's tail behind it.

Villa was watching from the front seat of the car. 'The salt's too wet to go mucking about like this,' he said, shaking his head. 'You can't play games on this stuff.' But most of us were elated. The sun was shining, the salt was drying, *Bluebird* was running at last. We stopped the car at the three-mile mark and waited for her to return.

'How long for her to get up to three hundred?' Wally Parr asked Norris. He had his notebook with him, and the designer gave a cautious reply.

'Some time. Ten days perhaps. Don must get thoroughly at home with the controls, and there's still a lot we need to find out about the old car. We'll want as many runs as we can get from now on.'

He spoke flatly, as if there was nothing to get worked up about, and he scratched the tip of his nose where it had caught the sun.

Campbell must have turned the car under her own power and made the return run almost immediately, for *Bluebird* reappeared four or five minutes later. This time she was moving.

'That's well over two hundred,' said Villa, shaking his head again.

The salt cloud behind the car looked larger this time, especially at one point where the water was holding longer than in the rest of the track, and the car seemed to quiver slightly as it struck it.

But *Bluebird* was travelling. That was what mattered. It was so effortless that the gloom of the last few days appeared hysterical and quite ridiculous.

We drove back to the base camp. By the time we reached it *Bluebird* was at rest outside the tank shelter, and the canopy was already open, sticking up like a marker arrow from the front of the car. Campbell was still in the cockpit, but he had taken his helmet off and was talking to Tonia who was leaning over the side of the car holding Whacko and the crash helmet.

It was strange how his face had changed. The lines on his forehead had gone. The face itself was fuller. He looked younger, suddenly assertive, and his eyes seemed to have lost that strange, lifeless pallor. He was enjoying the one rightful function of his life at last and everyone around him knew it.

'We were up to two hundred and twenty on the second run on less than twenty-five per cent power,' he said for the benefit of the people crowding around the cockpit. In the weeks to come I was to recognise the clipped, impersonal voice he reserved for such announcements as these, but at that moment, since everything was so dominated by mood, life seemed suddenly very simple. A few days at the most. A few days and the car would be up to the record. A few days and the gamble would have paid off. For in a curious way this car had already come to represent something more than the ambition of the man who owned her. All of us were involved in her now. Cut off from the rest of the world, isolated in the middle of this unearthly lake, nothing else had meaning. Failure now would be the failure of us all, and just for the moment it seemed as if we were gambling everything we stood for on its success.

Villa asked suddenly if there were to be any more runs that day, and Campbell nodded and lit himself a cigarette. 'Two more, Unc. There and back. Then we must see about something to eat.'

It all seemed a matter of routine at the time. All of us helped swing the car round, backing her in a great arc, and when the canopy had closed, the buzzer sounded and the engine whirred and thundered, the ritual had already become familiar. Most of us stayed behind at the camp this time, and saw the car turn away and head straight on to the glare of the main track. It went swifter than ever. The acceleration of the car was phenomenal, and it was only when it was almost on the horizon that I saw the cloud of spray behind the car was larger than before.

Carl Noble was sitting up on the top of the army wrecker truck, watching through a pair of field-glasses.

'Salt,' he shouted down, 'only salt. It's the sun makes it look more than it is.'

On this run *Bluebird* took longer to return, and when she did appear she was travelling more slowly than before. Campbell was subdued when he lifted the canopy. 'Only a hundred and thirty that time,' he said.

The inspection covers had been lifted off the engine and oil temperatures were being taken.

'Ken,' said Campbell to Ken Norris, who was busily noting down the readings in his brown file. 'As soon as you've finished I think we'd better take a look at that track.'

The meters inside the car give most of the readings Norris needs for his calculations, including engine revolutions, jet pipe temperature, maximum impact on the front suspension, and brake line pressures.

'Don, d'you realise that you recorded one point eight G on your suspension that time?' said Norris, looking suddenly perturbed. 'You must have hit something one hell of a whack.'

'Ken, leave that and come up and have a look at the track,' said Campbell quietly.

We took the grey Valiant saloon with the silencer sawn off specially for work on the lake. The whole bodywork was now caked in the white and rust coloured salt, making it look as if it had been delicately iced.

Campbell drove. Although nothing had been said, all the optimism and elation had already gone. So great is Campbell's power of conveying a mood.

We stopped at the four-mile mark. 'I think this is the place,' he said, speaking for the first time. 'Something very odd happened here.'

We got out and strolled over to the fifty-yard-wide ribbon of track which the graders had smoothed until it was like a great motorway running to the north. But although it was smooth, the surface was thin, and I remembered what Leo Villa had said. 'By mid-afternoon the heat of the sun will draw the water up through the salt, so that instead of drying in the heat it'll get wetter.'

This was what was happening now, and there in the middle of the course were *Bluebird*'s tracks. They ran for a hundred yards each way where the wheels had ploughed three-inch deep furrows through the slush. Already these furrows had filled with water.

'Crikey,' said Campbell, staring down at one of the furrows and digging at the wet salt crystals with the toe of his boot. 'Crikey.'

Norris started pacing out the length of the ruts. 'One hundred and fifty yards,' he shouted.

Someone else measured the depth of the water. 'Three inches.'

'Three inches, Skipper,' said Villa. 'You've only got four inches clearance on the car. You realise how near you were to scraping your belly on the bloody deck?'

'That explains your one point eight G, Ken old boy,' said Campbell. 'On the return journey I got my wheels into the ruts I had made on the third run. It was just like getting your wheels in the tramlines at the Elephant and Castle on a wet Saturday night.'

By now two more trucks had joined us, and all along the track were melancholy men staring at the ruts, testing the salt with their feet and advancing their own theories of how long it would take to make the track usable again.

'You realise, Skipper, that this is slap up the middle of your course?' said Villa. 'You can't do a thing till you've got this little lot cleared up.'

'I'll bring the light grader along first thing tomorrow morning,' said the large young man who worked with the team preparing the track. 'Soon fill up those ruts for you with loose salt. You'll be surprised how quick this salt heals.'

But even as he spoke all of us knew it could not be as simple as that. We had left the world of precise difficulties that engineers could do something about. We were up against more mysterious disasters. The surface of Lake Eyre was not something that could be repaired like a torn engine cowling.

'I think,' said Campbell, turning back towards the car, 'that there are still certain things we need to find out about this course before we try any further runs on it.'

4
The Main Track Dies

From the air Campbell's problem was very clear. From six thousand feet in the bright sunlight of the following morning Lake Eyre was immaculate—smooth surfaced, the salt golden, the horizon never-ending. But when the ailerons dipped and the note of the engine rose and Campbell brought the Aero Commander down to a few hundred feet, turning and banking to the east of the main camp, the salt seemed to change.

It was no longer clear. It varied from one point to another. There were dark grey patches where the water was near the surface, and lighter areas where the salt skin was down to an inch or two. And even where the salt looked thick and hard there was trouble.

'Salt islands everywhere this year,' shouted Campbell, shaking his head grimly. 'Never seen them like this before.'

And for mile after mile they stretched, these strange circular blemishes like a rash across the salt. They were another of the oddities of Lake Eyre. For the salt was growing all the time as the water evaporated, and as the crystals built up they would form around anything—the body of a bird or a rabbit. Even a leaf or a blade of grass would be enough to start with. It would take some months before the salt island was noticeable, but it would go on growing until it was like the scab of an immense ulcer feeding off the flat surface of the salt. Sometimes it might reach twelve hundred feet in diameter, and its rim could be twelve inches high.

If any fell across *Bluebird*'s track they would need to be levelled. This took time for they were tough, with a solid core of rock salt hard enough to repel the heaviest grader. When the main track was being prepared Campbell had developed a sort of portable milling machine which actually ground the salt islands away until they were level with the rest of the salt. But a single island could take up to a couple of days to remove, and if we were to find an alternative track there would be no time at all for this. Somehow we had to find a pathway fifteen miles long with hard salt all the way which led *between* the islands. To ask for this was like asking for a straight path through the Milky Way.

Another thing we could appreciate from the aircraft was how well Mustard had chosen the line for the main track. Apparently he had photographed the southern end of the lake from the air and then used the photographs to make a map on which to calculate the one ideal route with the hardest salt and the least number of islands. The only trouble was that the southern end of the lake was now draining straight into it.

'It looks like it's got to be the old main track or nothing,' said Campbell as he headed the aircraft back towards Muloorina. He was tense and stared straight ahead. His words were meant for no one but himself.

'What do you do if it stays as it was yesterday?' I asked.

'I shudder to think, old boy.'

Although I had never met Andrew Mustard, I recognised the angular, red-bearded figure in the light-blue overalls of the *Bluebird* team at once. He was waiting by the airstrip as we landed. Campbell treated him, I noticed, circumspectly.

'Well, Andy? Good trip back?'

'Thank you, Donald. Yes, I was driving the Humber. Just over seven hours from Adelaide.'

'That's fantastic, Andy. You must have jolly nearly killed yourself.'

Mustard smiled and put his hands behind his back. 'Not quite, Donald. Not quite.'

'We had a run yesterday.'

'So I've heard.'

'Family all right, Andy?'

'Fine, Donald, thank you. Fine.'

There was a pause while the two men looked at each other. They were both Scots, but it would have been hard to pick a more total pair of opposites. Mustard, a meditative man, a believer, profoundly serious, with large brown eyes and not an ounce of spare flesh on him, and Campbell, a head shorter and a couple of stone heavier, opinionated, extrovert, a person who acted first and worried about it a long time afterwards.

But there was one great bond between them—*Bluebird*. Both of them were passionately involved in it. Possibly Mustard was the more emotional of the two about the car. For it was indisputably Campbell's own car. Mustard was only its reserve driver, and no one was even sure what that meant.

At the moment his chief responsibilities at Lake Eyre were to look after *Bluebird*'s tyres and wheels on behalf of the Dunlop Company who had made them, and to prepare the track. On this last task he had been working like a maniac throughout the previous months, and he had inspired great loyalty from the men who worked with him. Each morning they had been up at four-thirty and slaved on the course through the great heat of the Australian summer.

But Andrew Mustard had never kept it secret that his ambition was to drive *Bluebird*.

'You know, Ken,' he had once said to Norris, 'I'd give my right ball to drive that car.'

So far the sacrifice had not been demanded of him. As long as Campbell had his way, it never would be. *Bluebird*'s reserve driver had in fact never driven the car, even on a practice run.

'That track of yours, Andrew,' said Campbell at last. 'It's in a terrible state up around the seven-mile mark.'

'That was to be expected after last Friday's rain,' replied Mustard in an even voice, which seemed to irritate Campbell.

'We've already had to look for an alternative anyhow,' said Campbell sharply.

'I know you have. But I'm not sanguine, Donald. I'm not sanguine.'

'Well, what the hell do we do then?'

'You wait, Donald. You wait until it dries. There's nothing else you can do.'

Wait we did, throughout the rest of that week, with the tired, addictive boredom of the outback. You could hunt for small scorpions under the stones behind the homestead. You could wade along the creek observing the geese and ibises and doleful pelicans fishing among the reeds. You could watch the windpump and the sunset. You could poison the dingoes with Elliot Price.

Whatever you did seemed to bring the record no nearer, and without the record there was no escape.

This waiting game was bad for Campbell. It brought out his edginess, his lack of inner resources. He is a man who becomes miserable with nothing to do. He talked of flying up towards Alice Springs for the day but nothing came of it, and he spent his mornings playing a form of patience called Russian boule and his afternoons cleaning his guns—a .22 Winchester and a pair of very smart Spanish .32 automatics bought in Adelaide.

A change had come over him in the last few days. Whatever hopes he had had of a quick, exciting run at the record had gone completely. He knew how little chance of success there was, and he was convinced that something was against him. There was a touch of hopelessness about the way he pottered around the house in his blue blazer, waiting with dull persistence for the chance he needed.

It was a bad time for Tonia too. Muloorina was not for her, and she hated the boredom of waiting.

'They're always the same, these record bids,' she said, 'always straightforward until we get there. But he's worried this time—deep down he's really worried, and there's nothing I can do for him. I'd like to tell him to pack it up, but that's one thing he must never suspect. You see, I have to be his pal and I have to humour him. I mustn't nag or worry or have any doubts about what he's doing as any ordinary wife would. He's had two wives already and the record business finished them. So I must be different.'

Only once, while we were waiting, did Campbell show any sign of the bitterness he was feeling. It was on the Friday night and he was sitting opposite me in Elliot Price's large green armchair beneath the three china seagulls flying along the wall on their eternal journey towards the mantelpiece.

'It should be all right,' he mused. 'That bloody main track should be all right. Andrew Mustard has spent five thousand pounds of my money preparing it.'

He puffed at his pipe and looked suddenly old and rather lost, hunched as he was in his chair.

'Still, we'll know the truth tomorrow. I'm giving it a couple of runs at eight a.m. That should tell us whether we're properly in the soft and sticky.'

Saturday dawned, a clear golden morning such as you get only in the Australian outback in the early winter, and as we flew out to the lake it seemed to welcome us—a gala lake, clear and cold, shell pink and lilac. That morning it had the perfection of something just created.

There were even a few spectators waiting this time as the aircraft landed, and some relatives of Elliot Price who had driven across in a cream-coloured Ford Zephyr.

The film people were out in strength, the cameramen setting up their tripods for a last-minute interview with Campbell before the run. Isolated as we had been in the desert with this anxious man, we had forgotten that the world outside was interested in him too.

There was no chance of a record yet, no chance even of any great speed. But *Bluebird* is dangerous enough to be exciting whenever she runs, and beneath the excitement a few of us knew the truth. That the main track was having its final trial. If it failed this morning we would know that it was useless, and that Campbell's chances of getting the record were over.

But all this was hidden behind a great burst of efficiency preceding the run. Everyone was caught up in it. Andrew Mustard's men on the track were wearing new, immaculate white overalls for the first time. The name 'Andrew Mustard Limited' was printed in red script diagonally across the back, with underneath, in smaller letters, 'Lake Eyre, 1964'.

Mustard was nervous. Whether he liked it or not, his reputation depended on what happened to the car seven miles up on the track. He seemed preoccupied and spoke to no one except to give the occasional order to his men.

But quite apart from Mustard's team, all Campbell's party was out in force—Leo Villa with his sunglasses, Ken Norris in his maroon shirt, his brown folder under his arm, and the specialist engineers from the different companies associated with Campbell on the record bid—Scrimshire of Motor Panels, like some old Viking chieftain, Reaks of Smith's Instruments, with his large moustache, and Carl Noble of Electro-Hydraulics in an old pair of *Bluebird* team overalls which he had worn at Utah in 1960.

'Okay. Roll her out,' shouted Campbell, and all of us went to help.

It was still early, not eight yet, but the light was diamond hard and shone brilliantly on the clean-cut lines of the car.

Campbell stood on his own, looking lost and forgotten as he always did before a run. There was nothing for him to do until the moment when he had to risk his life, and none of us could help him.

I found myself near him and was suddenly embarrassed that he was risking his neck and I was not. It was a barrier between us. All I could think of saying was how beautiful the car was.

He nodded. 'Except for those bloody great wheels,' he said. 'You know how big they are? Fifty-two inches in diameter. Just think how much better she would look with smaller wheels. Ken did a beautiful job fitting them into the car, but I've always thought they ruin the look of the thing.'

He paused and lit himself a cigarette. 'It was those wheels that nearly did for me in Utah. Once you get into a spin with wheels that size, you've had it.'

For a moment it was as if he was talking to himself. Then he realised that he had said too much, and walked off without another word to join Tonia.

She always managed to be unflustered, slightly casual with him before a run—very much the pal now, no sign of the worried wife. It was an admirable performance. She was wearing black and white check slacks and a silk sweater, and her hair was tied with a white ribbon. As far as the newspapers were concerned she was simply 'Tonia Bern, cabaret singer', but she was more that that. She was a woman of character. She had common sense, and she was practical and clever enough to keep her fears to herself.

They talked for a few minutes. Then she gave him his mascot and his helmet and his oxygen mask. He slid himself on to the side of the cockpit, then she took his boots and handed him the blue tennis shoes. The operating-theatre routine of starting up began as Campbell and Norris started their last check.

'Master switch—on.'

'Accelerometer—on.'

'Check breathing air.'

'Gearbox pumps—pressures correct.'

Campbell's voice was muffled now, coming from deep within the car, and although the cockpit cover was still open, it was already the voice of someone about to be cast off—a diver before his helmet is bolted down, a spaceman before communications cease.

The lid went down. The buzzer sounded again as it had sounded four days before. Once again the engine whirred then roared to life, and the turbine lashed out with its power, sending the smoke and the heat freckling across the salt.

As *Bluebird* moved off, Wally Parr was busily taking photographs with a small camera of his own. He seemed uncomfortable to be caught doing anything so unprofessional. 'For the family album,' he said. 'Thought it worth taking a few happy snaps. After all, she's the last of these things we're likely to see.'

'By the way,' he added, 'has he been talking to you too about the Utah crash? It's odd. You'd think he'd want to forget a thing like that.'

The brilliance of the light on the lake foreshortened every distance, and the heat haze was so intense that by eleven o'clock in the morning the horizon came down to about a mile. At two hundred yards a car appeared to float in mid-air. At a quarter of a mile a tent began to form a quavering mirror image beneath it. And at a mile it would be swallowed up in the glare where the lake surface and the sky joined in a permanent arc of light. This made the lake a terrifying place to get lost on, and added to the unearthliness of Campbell's runs at speed.

One moment the car was in front of you in that hard white light that permitted no shadows and made it seem the most tangible thing in the world. Then as the turbine roared the salt spurted from the wheels, the sun flashed on the great tail, and *Bluebird* was away, swifter than any rocket. This was not a car being driven. It was a launching into outer space, a conjuring trick where speed and light and silence and distance were all there to deceive the senses.

Campbell was the only person for whom *Bluebird*'s journey could have any reality. For him, in his cockpit, there was the flashing past of the big coloured canvas markers at each mile, and the wide blue dye line running up the centre of the track for him to steer by. For the four or five minutes of a run he had his dials to watch, the rate of acceleration to take care of, and the certainty that if anything did go wrong it would all be over before he could do very much about it. At three hundred miles an hour in the half-second between his senses noticing, his mind reacting, his arm or leg moving and the controls functioning, the car would have travelled through two hundred and twenty feet. A spin, a skid, a sudden loss of control, and the moment from Utah which he seemed unable to forget would be repeating itself somewhere up there amid the glare and the mirages of the lake.

That morning there was a long wait after *Bluebird* had roared off into the distance, and when the car finally reappeared it came so slowly that we knew at once something was wrong. Campbell slid the car to a halt, lifted the cockpit cover, and sat there, silent and slightly dazed.

'Well, Skipper?' said Villa at last.

'It's no good,' said Campbell, handing him the crash helmet. 'No good at all. I put on less than twenty-five per cent power and the wheels went right through the surface just beyond the seven-mile mark. Exactly the same as the other day. It's not going to dry out, and there's no question of further runs on it, Unc. You couldn't ride a bicycle safely on it at the moment.'

So it was all over. He sat there in the cockpit and no one spoke because there was nothing to say, but Tonia had the sense to get his boots from him and tell him there was coffee in the hangar and it was getting cold.

He clambered out then. The news photographers took the pictures they needed to go with their reports on Campbell calling off an attempt for the second year running. The newsreel camera-man stopped him and said, 'Hold it, Donald. Just a moment if you would. We'd like a good shot of you looking depressed.'

Campbell smiled wearily, and all he said was, 'I suppose I must look as I feel.'

He walked away not towards the hangar, but to the grey Valiant and once in the car, sitting at the wheel, his calm began to crack.

'Bloody place. Filthy bloody place,' he said under his breath, and slammed his foot on the accelerator. The wheels spun on the salt and we jerked forward down the service road. Suddenly he swung straight on to the middle of the main track and raced down it at ninety, following the wheel marks *Bluebird* had left twenty minutes before.

'No need to worry about this any more.' He was beginning to shout now.

'Fifteen miles of uselessness. Six months' work. I don't know how many thousand quids' worth of machinery, and you end up with precisely nothing.'

We stopped, and all trooped silently from the car at a point where the ruts were very deep. There was no point in Ken Norris pacing them out this time or measuring them. They seared into the track from one end to the other. The salt everywhere was wet and crumbling.

For a while Campbell looked down at the track, his face grey in the bright sun and the tears running down his cheeks. The sunlight glinted on the neat row of salt crystals the wheels had banked on each side of the ruts. The sky was very blue.

He had waited nine years for this moment, and now there was nothing to be said and nothing to be done except get back into the car and drive home.

5
The Search

'And now all you South Australians, the time is six-fifteen and this is the news from the ABC read by Ralph Binns. On Lake Eyre today, British record breaker Donald Campbell had two trial runs on his specially prepared track and found the surface of the salt so softened after recent rains that he was unable to get above one-eighty miles an hour. Campbell said afterwards that he thought things were hopeless, and he is expected to postpone his bid for the world land speed record until September.'

So that was that.

'Quite right too,' said Elliot Price, leaning forward to turn off the radio. 'He'll kill himself if he goes on here. Come September the lake'll be dried out real proper, but you can't expect the man to go ahead with the salt in the state it is now.'

'That's the end then,' said Wally Parr. 'He can't postpone again. This was his last chance, and if he leaves now he might as well give *Bluebird* to the Science Museum and pack up for good.'

'I don't see why,' said Elliot. 'September'd be fine. The car's all right and the man's all right. It's just a case of waiting and having trust in Donald to pull it off when the lake's in better shape.'

But although nobody argued with the old man, most of us knew that Parr was probably right. A record breaker is good for only so many failures, and Campbell had exceeded his quota. There would not be the money or the enthusiasm or the time or the energy for another go in September. The record had to be now or never.

The news of the postponement spread quickly and produced a strange mood of light-heartedness within the camp. This was not from any particular animosity against Campbell. At this point he was still popular enough. It was simply that people had had enough of Muloorina and enough waiting around doing nothing. It was a luxury to have a decision at last. Whatever the disappointment for Campbell, it was impossible not to be glad it was over.

Because of this there was a touch of guilt behind the sympathy we showed for Campbell when he appeared for dinner that evening. And as it turned out, the dinner was especially good.

'We don't want any food left behind this time,' Tonia had said as she drove back that afternoon from the lake. 'Last year we had to pull out in such a hurry after the rains came that we had to leave behind fifty pounds' worth of provisions.'

So that night we were eating what would otherwise have been wasted, but the meal had something of a celebration about it all the same.

There was asparagus soup—good, thick, Belgian soup with small drops of fat glistening on the surface, and large chunks of tinned asparagus added. And there was steak and broad beans and boiled potatoes and fried potatoes, and most of us ate with a sort of weary relief that the whole thing was over. We were hungry after the day on the lake, and by eating well and asking for second helpings of the tough, metallic-tasting rump meat which was the best the cattle could make out of this dead, grey land, we were showing ourselves that there was more to life than Lake Eyre.

Campbell sat at the head of the table as usual, and to start with one attempted to avoid his eye for it was wrong to be happy about something which spelled the end of all he had worked for. But he looked cheerful enough himself, and it was impossible to believe that this was the same man who stood in the middle of Lake Eyre ten hours before, with tears running down his cheeks, cursing the day he had ever set eyes on the place.

When he is in good spirits, Campbell is unbeatable. He has a wonderful verbal memory. He tells stories with a great schoolboy's gusto and never stops laughing at his own jokes. For some reason he was in good spirits that night.

It was only his eyes that gave him away, and you had to know him well to notice it. But just occasionally there would be a certain look when he stopped talking and had not quite begun to laugh. For a moment the eyes opened a fraction wider than usual, and seemed to see nothing.

But most of the time he talked, and talked better than I had ever heard him. He told us about Tahiti, and about the south of France and how a couple of years before he had hired a yacht from Antibes. One evening, moored off Juan les Pins, he had had a visitor.

'Strapping great fellow, he was. Six foot six, blond hair, monocle screwed firmly into the left eye. He hauled himself up over the side naked as the day he was born. Came on deck, put his heels together, bowed and said "You are Herr Donald Campbell. I am General von something-or-other. I have long wished for the pleasure of your acquaintance."

'Well. What could I do? Decidedly tricky. Never met a naked general before. So I said, "Have a drink, old boy." And while we were drinking our brandy and sodas the general suddenly said, "Excuse me, Herr Campbell, but I have two friends who also wish to make your acquaintance."

'"Certainly," I said. "We must arrange a meeting sometime." "That will not be necessary," he replied. "They are here now," and he leant over the side of the boat, shouted something in German, and two young girls who must have been swimming around all this time came to the side of the boat and clambered aboard.

'Very attractive girls they were, and just like the general—not a stitch. Not a bloody stitch between them. Well, we were formally introduced, and had another drink. We chatted for a while. Then twenty minutes later the general stood up, said, "Thank you Herr Campbell. Now it is time for dinner." And before I could ask him to stay, he and the two girls had gone to the side of the boat, dived back into the water, and started swimming off in the direction of Juan. Never saw them again.'

When the steak was finished there was apple pie and custard. Campbell likes apple pie and his spirits seemed to improve still further at the sight of it. Even Leo Villa, who had started dinner with the face of an old priest preparing for a funeral, began to catch his mood and started to cheer up. He talked for a while about some of the early record breakers of before the war.

'Segrave. Now he was very good. And Parry Thomas. Your father had some battles with him in his time, Donald.'

'I'll never forget the day he was killed,' said Campbell. 'Father was home and lunch was a very silent meal that day.'

After the apple pie there were cigars and Scotch whisky and more stories from Campbell. Nothing seemed able to quench his absurdly good spirits. Andrew Mustard came in to see what was going on.

Mustard was looking very serious. He had spent six months on that main track, and inevitably his reputation had been involved in it.

'Sit down, Andy. Whisky? Cigar? Or would you prefer some brandy? It's Australian, but I can personally recommend it.'

'Thank you, Donald, some whisky.' There was silence as Mustard chose himself a cigar, and when it was alight he looked at Campbell and said, 'Well, Donald?'

'Well, Andy,' said Campbell. 'It looks like one of those things, doesn't it.'

After dinner that night there was another meeting of the entire team up in the old shearers' quarters, and everyone was there to hear Campbell speak his own epitaph.

'It's going to be interesting to hear how he phrases it,' said Wally Parr, taking out his notebook as Campbell arrived. 'And I want to hear what our friend Mustard has to say for himself.'

'Good evening, gentlemen,' said Campbell. He stood for a few seconds waiting for the conversations to die away, a solid, suddenly impassive figure, puffing at what was left of his cigar. In the half-hour since dinner he had changed yet again. He was tense now and deadly serious. He was standing almost directly beneath the light which showed up the small bald patch at the back of his head. The room became suddenly very silent.

'Gentlemen. There was a report on the radio tonight that I am postponing the attempt until September. I have no idea how such a report reached the Australian Broadcasting Corporation, but I would like to say here and now that it is totally and utterly incorrect. Nothing is being postponed. Today was a disappointment. A bitter disappointment. But nothing, I repeat nothing, is being postponed.'

He paused, and the smoke from his cigar swirled up against the light. The only sound in the room was the noise of Parr's pencil as he took down the statement for the benefit of next morning's papers.

'The other day, fearing this might happen, several of us made an aerial reconnaissance to look for a possible alternative to the present main track. We saw what looked like a possible area to the east. It is clear after this morning's run that the present main track is not going to be in a condition to take *Bluebird* during the foreseeable future, so we must find somewhere that will. The search will commence tomorrow morning at first light. I will fly in the Aero Commander, and I will need as much support as I can have from the ground. The procedure will be as follows. I will select what looks like a possible route from the air. I will signal by dipping the wings of the aircraft and the cars can follow. We will need your co-operation in this, gentlemen, and I would be grateful for as many as possible of you with your cars on the lake tomorrow morning.

'I need hardly add that time is of the essence in this entire operation. The situation is desperate. It need not be impossible. Are there any questions?'

Parr asked about arrangements for track preparations once a new course was found. 'If the present main track took six months to prepare, how long will it be before you are ready to run even if you do find the sort of area you need?'

'That, Wally, is a problem we must meet when we come to it. I know how much time and effort the present main track cost. It also took a great deal of my money. I was never entirely convinced that the track should have been prepared that far in advance of the record attempt.'

If Mustard had been going to speak, this was his cue. He was sitting on one of the iron bedsteads, wearing a blue blazer and a white shirt with a floppy collar and a blue silk club tie. But he kept silent.

'Right, gentlemen,' said Campbell. 'Lake Eyre, at seven a.m. tomorrow morning.'

If it had not been for the meal and the cigars and the story about the German general, it is just possible he might not have got away with it. Before we went to dinner that night most of us had been convinced that there was no hope and were anxious to get away. But things were different now. He had established contact with us over dinner. We had eaten with him and drunk his whisky and laughed at his stories, and if he wanted to go on looking for another track there was not a great deal we could do about it now.

The journey to the lake was nearly thirty miles, and on the road it took most drivers three-quarters of an hour as they cornered and skidded across the ruts and potholes and drifts of stifling red bull-dust. The trek had begun at sunrise with every car available—the official Humber with 'Bluebird Project, Lake Eyre 1964' in heavy white lettering on the side, the hired cream-coloured Fords, the big grey Valiants, the battered Land Rover—all jolting down the track from the homestead as the sun came up, past the leafless coolibahs, bone white above the creek, past the wattle thickets with the flocks of grey and red parakeets, past the gum trees with the mud nests of the epicoma caterpillars swinging from the branches like heavy grey udders.

Ahead lay a fantastic landscape. The cars were trailing great streamers of dust, and the land each side was as flat and as empty as if it had been scraped with an immense steel ruler.

Most wildlife had been destroyed. Kangaroos were a rarity by day, although sometimes in the distance you could see a pair of emus racing away as you approached.

A few miles from the lake the landscape changed, and where the road the army built ran alongside the edge of the lake it was like approaching the shores of the Dead Sea. On the right were strange formations of sandstone eroded by the wind until they could have been the ruined fortress walls of some forgotten civilisation. And to the left of the road were the first layers of the mud surrounding the lake, mud that had cracked and wrinkled and corrugated and set into a hundred different textures, grey and red mud, with here and there the faintest silvering of salt.

We bumped our way over the causeway. The number of vehicles across it had already ploughed up the far end, and the lake itself was more than ever like a lake of ice, with the salt churning up like snow crystals.

At the base camp Villa and the mechanics were working away at the car again. However slender were the chances now that *Bluebird* could ever run, it was typical of him to keep to perfection.

Campbell too was there, a keen, decisive Campbell with large notebook and binoculars and several compasses. He also had his haversack which he had picked up the habit of carrying from his father whenever he was in rough country. It contained string, knife, brandy, water-bottle, and a revolver which fired small shot in case of snakes.

'Now you know what we want,' he said. 'Smooth, hard salt, devoid of salt islands.' And when he had issued the compasses, he gave us bearings to follow and told us that wherever we found anything we should halt the car and wait until the aircraft came over.

He has a great knack of arranging plans, organising expeditions, giving orders. He once told me that what he always wanted to be as a boy was an army officer. The OTC was one of the few things he had really enjoyed at school at Uppingham, and when we had all received our compasses and our instructions and were ready to go, there was a distinct air of a school field day about it all.

'Don't forget,' shouted Campbell, giving us all one last piece of advice, 'if you get lost, stick with the car. We'll soon spot you from the air, but once you go wandering off on your own, there's a chance we won't see you again.'

One by one the cars fanned out eastwards, trying to find what no one except Campbell believed could be found—a clear stretch of salt, fourteen miles long, hard enough to bear not just the weight of *Bluebird*, but the force of its great wheels as they kicked with all the power of that five thousand horse-power engine at four hundred miles an hour.

As soon as we were away from the camp, Lake Eyre took over. At the base camp, as Campbell gave his orders in that precise young army officer's voice of his, it had all seemed straightforward. But less that ten minutes later, as I continued on my course of 290 degrees east, I realised that I was utterly lost. The trouble was the very brightness of the lake. In this gleaming white world there was not a landmark to set a compass by, and all you could do was drive on, trying to follow your senses, but knowing all the time that you were veering constantly from one way to the other. On their own the senses are deceptive, and all the time there were mirages which sprang up above the salt islands, looking like cars or tents or groups of people, only to vanish as you got closer.

Once I passed a duck which must have been blown on to the lake. It rose weakly as the car approached, flew a few yards, and then flopped on to the wet salt again. By midday the sun would have finished it off. Within a few weeks it would be starting a salt island of its own.

Even from the air I had not realised how much the surface of the salt varied. At one point it would be so wet that water swished and spurted from the wheels and the car left deep runnels behind it. Half a mile on, and I was threading my way between small, tightly packed salt islands. A little later there were small tufts to the salt, an inch or so high, that crunched like glass beneath the wheels. And every so often came the salt Campbell needed if he was to get his record—hard, smooth, impermeable salt, with a surface like perfectly laid concrete. There would be a patch, then just as it seemed that we had found what we needed, the wheels struck the wet again.

I had been driving like this for more than half an hour when I spotted the small blue and white aircraft circling away to the left, and although I lost sight of it, it gave me the direction I needed, and I drove over. It is surprising how fast a car can travel on this salt when it has to. But Campbell had landed already by the time I got there.

The aircraft was on one of the hard patches of salt, and Campbell was talking to Ken Norris, who had driven one of the other cars. He looked excited, more decisive and clear-cut than ever. He had put on a red and white choker, and was trying to pick a hole in the salt with the end of his clasp knife.

'Well, old boy, if it's anywhere it's here,' he said. 'It's pretty rough in places, but it runs for eight miles before it gets soft again and it's free of salt islands.'

'But eight miles?' I said. 'What use is that?'

'Well, it's a start for heaven's sake. There's a lot we can do with eight miles.'

'But you can't get the record with that length.'

'At least I can get the car moving. That will be something, and afterwards you never know. There may be a chance of squeezing another mile or two each end when the salt has dried out a bit.'

'But you need fourteen miles of flat, hard salt.'

'Can't be too choosy now, old boy. If I have to try and make do with less, I'm afraid it'll be just too bad.'

And by now I had been on Lake Eyre long enough to know

what that would mean. Neither a yes nor a no. Just the slenderest of chances, the most tantalising of possibilities which the lake was offering now to keep us here. For already I thought of the lake as a person—cunning, beautiful, malignant, with moods that were always changing and an intelligence which was going to extract the greatest pleasure out of tormenting Donald Campbell before it finally destroyed him.

6

Point of No Return

From where Campbell was standing at the eastern end of his new track, the small black outline of the Land Rover scarcely seemed to move and the silence of the lake was so total that while it was still a long way off we could hear the noise of the engine and the strangely lulling, crunching sound of the big steel drag ironing down the roughness of the salt.

'It's a slow business, Andy,' said Campbell.

'It is indeed,' said Mustard.

Slowly the Land Rover advanced towards us. It began to look like some hard-shelled inexorable insect.

'Is it nearly done now?' asked Campbell.

'It's getting as good as we can reasonably hope for. If we smooth it away much further we're likely to destroy the hardest part of the surface and there's water only a few inches down.'

This was the fifth day of work on the new track, and while the rest of the camp had been waiting back at Muloorina the two Land Rovers had been out on the empty lake from dawn to dusk plying their way backwards and forwards along the eight miles of the new course. They never exceeded five miles an hour. Several times the welded steel joints between the steel rails of the drags had come apart and precious hours were lost while they were laboriously repaired. On the Sunday, rain was forecast, and although it never fell a belt of felt-grey rain-cloud hung over the west of the lake for the next couple of days.

But now on Wednesday 13 May, the work was nearly done. The clouds had gone. It looked as if *Bluebird* would soon have a chance to run again. Campbell seemed cheerful, almost excited this morning. He was polite to Andrew Mustard.

'They seem to have done a great job, your chaps, Andy—a great job.'

He kicked the salt with his heel and nodded approvingly when he saw that it made scarcely an impression. 'If the rest of the track is as good as this, I think we'll really be getting somewhere.'

Mustard was wearing white overalls and canvas shoes. He looked tall and angular beside the squatter, more solid figure of Campbell. The wind ruffled the hair away from the smooth bald dome above his forehead. His eyes were hidden behind rimless sunglasses, and it was hard to see how he was reacting to Campbell's praise.

'Well, Donald, I would suggest that we don't overlook the fact that this end, the northern extremity of the course, possesses much the most satisfactory surface.' His diction was precise, professorial—his thought guarded.

'Farther south it begins to deteriorate a fraction, but on the whole I think you should find the course will meet your minimal requirements.'

'You do, do you? Well, I think we should all have a quick look. Is that all right with you, gentlemen?'

'Fine, Skipper. Quite agree,' said Leo Villa.

'Yes,' said Ken Norris, nodding and biting his lower lip. Neither of them showed great enthusiasm for the new course, but if Campbell was happy that was something.

'Have you carried out adhesion tests on the new track yet?' said Norris to Mustard as we climbed into the grey Valiant saloon.

'But naturally, Kenneth. Naturally. Although I wouldn't attach too much credence to them at this stage of the game. Since the last rains the surface of the lake seems to be changing from one hour to the next. It is my considered opinion that all runs should take place as soon after first light as humanly possible. The effect of the sun is to draw the water towards the surface of the salt, making the lake progressively softer towards midday.'

Mustard gained confidence as he spoke. He seemed to relish being an expert, and the completion of this new track had worked wonders for his morale.

Campbell drove the Humber. He was wearing his red and white check neck-scarf and had started chewing spearmint. All his attention now was on the track.

This new track of his lay several miles to the east of the old main course, and at right angles to it. The only chance of extending it was to the west, but if this was done it would mean crossing the waterlogged surface of the old track at about the third-mile mark.

'Okay, everyone. Hold very tight,' shouted Campbell suddenly, and before we knew what was happening he had slammed on the brakes and locked the wheels. The Humber skidded to a halt.

Leo Villa pushed his spectacles back from the end of his nose.

'Phew, Skipper. What's the idea?'

'A little test, Leo, old boy. Now let's get out and measure the length of the skid marks. That ought to give us a rough guide to the adhesion value of the salt. Don't you think so, Ken?'

'Yes, I think we can work something out from that. What speed were we doing when you locked the brakes?'

'Thirty exactly.'

'Let's have a look at the skid marks then.'

We were about two miles from the start of the track and the salt was in good condition here. Even so, the very top layer of the salt was damp, and when we measured out the skid marks with the old leather-cased surveyor's tape Campbell kept in his haversack we found that it had taken the Humber thirty-five yards to stop.

'What d'you think of that, Ken?' asked Campbell sharply. 'Is it good enough for us?'

'Looks a bit dodgy to me, Don, but I'd like a few more figures to go on. D'you think you could repeat the performance at intervals along the track?'

Norris squatted uncomfortably with the large brown folder open on his knees.

'Don't forget, Donald,' said Mustard looking at his watch, 'the time is now eleven twenty-five. The lake is approaching its wettest period of the day. At first light you would get a better reading.'

'Point taken, Andy. But let's do as Ken suggests. It'll give us something to go on.'

So we spent the remaining eight miles accelerating, skidding and measuring. Ken Norris recorded the results in his folder without comment.

'Well,' said Campbell when we had reached the western end of the track. 'It's a course. I'll say that for it.'

He spat out his chewing-gum, lit a cigarette and blew the smoke thoughtfully between pursed lips.

'It still seems very rough, Andy, and this end is pretty wet. Are you sure you can't get it any smoother?'

'I could, Donald, but it would mean destroying the hardest part of the salt. The more we smooth it the wetter it gets.'

'Okay, Andy. We'll have to see what Ken's figures have to tell us. And thank your chaps for me. I think they've worked wonders.'

'My father?' said Campbell. 'Obviously he has been the most important single influence on my life, and you could come up with some very fancy Freudian theories to explain what I'm up to at Lake Eyre.'

Norris and Villa still had work to do on the car and had decided to stay on. Campbell and I drove back together in the Morris 1100.

'You must remember that I grew up in the shadow of the great man. He was a formidable person to have as a father. He was tough. Dynamic. Quite ruthless at getting anything he really wanted.'

From the point where we left the shores of the lake, the road had deteriorated into a series of bends and gullies often covered in drifts of yielding red dust. But Campbell handled each hazard with a sort of preoccupied neatness. The speed never dropped below seventy.

'Of course he had great charm too—a kind of boyish vitality and enthusiasm for anything he took on. In some ways he never stopped being a schoolboy. He liked the things boys like—cars, aeroplanes, gadgets of all sorts. You've heard all about his treasure hunting. In 1926, you know, he went off in search of Spanish treasure on Cocos Island in the Pacific. Went with his old chum Kennelm Lee Guinness, the man the KLG sparking plug was named after. The treasure was there all right. They located the position according to the old charts but they couldn't reach it. The Marquis of Bristol later discovered a cave but the roof had fallen in and the actual treasure was right under the sea. It's always been a great dream of mine to go back with drills and diving apparatus and have a crack at finding the old man's treasure. I'd get a great kick out of that.

'He used to take me poaching with him sometimes too when I was a kid. He was good for anything with a bit of adventure in it.'

We had reached the long straight stretch of track which succeeds the spectacular Dead Sea landscape bordering the lake. Campbell wound his window down and lit a cigarette as he drove.

'For me childhood was like growing up with an extraordinarily successful elder brother in the house. I think I reacted very much as younger brothers are supposed to in such circumstances. In some ways it held me back, made me unsure of myself. You remember asking me the other day why I never thought of going in for a record while my father was alive. Well, there was no question of it. In our family Father was the one who got the records.'

'I used to kick hard against the old man too. We fought. For crying out loud, we fought. He was such a character that you had to fight him or else go under completely.

'To make it worse, while I was trying hard to be like him—I aped him at one period, even tried to brush my hair the way he did—he was just as determined to turn me into everything he wasn't. "You know what your father would have been if he'd been born two hundred years earlier?" he used to say. "A pirate, boy. A pirate and a jolly good one too."

'But he didn't want me to be a pirate. He wanted me to be something respectable in the City. He tried very hard. I'll say that for Father, he tried.

'He was mean too—very tight about money. In 1925, for instance, old Leo had just got back to England after they'd set the new 300 mph land speed record and shoved in his expenses for the journey. Don't forget that in those days Leo was earning a few quid a week and working like a Trojan for it. All the same, Father went through the expenses with a tooth comb and saw an entry for oysters on Leo's celebration dinner. Out they came. "Why should I pay for oysters?" he said.'

By now we were at the bleak centre part of the journey, with the plain all round us as flat and limitless as an ocean of grey dust. He increased the speed and fell silent.

'And how did this strange relationship with your father affect you in the end?' I asked.

'I wouldn't know. That's for other people to say. I'm still trying to find the answers for myself.'

Campbell was cheerful that night at dinner, and as always his good humour was infectious. There was leek soup and cottage pie and carrots, and Elliot Price told the story of how his stomach fell through his diaphragm one afternoon when he was standing on his head to amuse his youngest grandchild.

'You've no idea of the pain, Don. Terrible. Terrible it was. If it hadn't been for Mother and the family I'd have asked the doctor to finish me off once and for all.'

'But what happened, Elliot? How did your guts land back in the right place?' asked Campbell.

'Well, Don. It's quite a story. Took me down to Adelaide they did. X-rayed me. Brought all the specialists in. Prodded me, shook me around and then told me that when I stood on my head the weight of my guts had split my diaphragm and wedged 'em up into my chest.

'"What are you going to do about it?" I asked 'em. "I'm in agony."

'"Well, Mr Price," they said, "we can operate but you'll only have a fifty-fifty chance of pulling through!"

'"Fifty-fifty, doctor," I said. "That's no good to me. If that's the best you can give me, I'm off."

'So back to Muloorina I come. Still in agony. Terrible agony. But at least I'm alive, you understand. Mother looks after me.'

'But, Elliot,' said Campbell, lighting a cigar, 'you still haven't told us how you got all those guts of yours back in the right place.'

'Give me time, Donald, give me time. What happens is as follows. For six months I'm in bed. The agony goes on. Can't keep any food down. I'm at the end of my tether. Then one night, after eleven it is, the policeman from over Marree arrives here, knocks on the door and shouts "Elliot. We needs help quick. There's bastard sheep stealers on your land."

'"Bastard sheep stealers," I said. "The bastards."

'"Yes," he shouts. "They're after your bastard sheep. What're you going to do about it, Elliot?"

'"I'm coming with you, constable," I says.

'"What, in your condition?"

'"Yes, in my condition. I've had enough of this lying in bed in agony. If I've got to go I'll go now, but so help me, I'll get those bastard sheep stealers first."

'So I take my gun and get in beside him in his big Dodge truck and away we go, driving like mad after these sheep stealers. It's black as pitch and the headlights aren't much good.

'Then suddenly it's like a flash of lightning hitting me, a great flash of pain that goes right through me, and I scream out with it.

'"Elliot," he says, shocked like. "Are you all right? We've bumped into a great hole in the track."

'"All right?" I says. "I'm finished. I'm going to die. Just leave

me there by the foot of that tree and get them bastard sheep stealers. That'll let me die happy."

'So he lies me down, gentle like, by the tree. And off he goes.
And somehow I don't die. I start feeling better instead. And an hour
later when the constable arrives back with the two bastard sheep
stealers expecting to be finding my corpse at the foot of the tree, he
sees me standing on my own two feet and as well as I am today.

'You see,' said the old man, leaning back in his chair and
grinning, 'it was the jolt that done it. Jolted my guts back down to
their rightful place again. And I never had trouble with them since.'

'But what did the doctors say when they saw you?' asked
Campbell.

'Well, you know what doctors are, Donald. They don't believe
anything they don't want to. But I always tell people that story
because I reckon there's a moral to it.'

'Perhaps there is, Elliot,' said Campbell, smiling and looking
straight at him with those pale eyes of his. 'Perhaps it means that
people of our age shouldn't go standing on our heads to amuse the
children.'

Now that Campbell had decided to try out his new track, Tonia
had a new worry, and after dinner she had a quiet word with Leo
Villa. He had always been a particular ally of hers, and she knew
there were things Campbell would confide in him that he would
never dream of telling her.

'Leo, it's really all right for tomorrow, isn't it?'

'All right? Lord, yes. Perfectly straightforward. The Skipper's
just doing a routine run to test out this new track.'

'Are you *sure* that's all he's going to do?' she said.

'Of course that's all he'll do. What else do you think could
happen?'

'I don't know. Perhaps it's silly of me, Leo, but I got the feeling
this afternoon that somehow Donald's attitude to the car was
changing. He seemed to have a sort of fever for it. You know how

he used to get like that sometimes with the boat, and how he was just before the crash at Utah.'

Villa looked at her quickly. 'There's nothing like that. I know him and I'd tell you if there was. All he's doing tomorrow is a slow run to try out the track.'

'D'you think he wants to kill himself?' asked Wally Parr at five to eight the following morning. Campbell's aircraft, blue and white, trim as ever, had just touched down on the lake, and we watched him step out of the small rectangular door beneath the wing, wave a brisk good-morning to Leo Villa, and then help down Tonia who handed him the ever-present blue leather holdall. He looked lively enough.

'I don't think so for a moment,' I said. 'If there's anyone who really enjoys life, it's Donald. And he is very cautious. If he were the suicidal type he'd have killed himself years ago.'

'Yes, I suppose so,' said Parr. 'We'd better take our pictures before he gets into *Bluebird*.' And both of us consulted light meters and set cameras before strolling across to where Campbell was already standing by the car. The ritual of these photographs was one of the more macabre touches of record breaking. People took then all the time because they always felt it necessary to have just one last picture of him in case anything happened.

Through the view-finder Campbell made a good picture as he stood talking to Ken Norris with the white salt and the sapphire blue of the car as a background. His profile is quite different from his full face. He looks stronger, more commanding, and as I focused the camera on him, the slightly beaked nose, the hard jawline, the sudden wrinkles as he screwed his eyes against the sun, reminded me of old photographs of his father from the early thirties.

'But the atmosphere of this morning's run is all wrong,' continued Parr as the shutter of his camera clicked. 'Things must be very desperate with him now. I just don't see what he can do with this eight-mile track, but he seems quite excited by it. Perhaps the old death wish is stronger than you think.'

Certainly Campbell was impatient to be off and the urgency of the occasion communicated itself to everyone. Andrew Mustard had been on the lake since before seven. He was at his most zealous, buzzing up and down the track in the tiny red Elfin racing car he used to test out the surface. He drove it with a sort of dedicated frenzy and after one last look at the track, came roaring up towards *Bluebird*, the engine crackling in a cloud of pale blue smoke.

Goggles glinting, crash helmet gleaming, salt in his red beard glistening, he leaned out of the cockpit to report the track clear and ready.

'It's all yours, Donald. It's flat and it's smooth.'

Campbell nodded. 'Fine. Fine, Andy,' and turned to Ken Norris. 'Recorder okay, Ken?'

'It's okay, Don.'

'Are you sure you remembered the coffee, darling?' he said to Tonia as she handed him his helmet. 'I missed my second cup at breakfast and I'll be ready for it when this is over.'

He winked at her, but she said nothing and took his crêpe-soled boots as he swung himself into the cockpit, then handed him the blue canvas shoes.

Because of the rush with which the new track had been laid, there had been no time to shift *Bluebird*'s hangar and the rest of the base camp across from the southern end of the old main track. Instead it was left where it was, and a new road had been graded which followed the old track for a couple of miles before turning right to meet the new track at the east.

Campbell took *Bluebird* up this road at a mere ninety. Several of us followed him in a cream-coloured Morris 1100. Tonia was with us, sitting in the back with her embroidery, Campbell's boots and Whacko the bear. She looked tense and nervous, which was unusual for her, and I saw that she had crumpled the corner of the linen she was embroidering and was still twisting it between her fingers.

The only time she spoke was when we were nearing the end of the service road and *Bluebird*, half a mile ahead of us, had begun to turn in a gentle arc to get on to the new track. It was exciting to see the car so close. As it turned, it did so with a great sense of power and purpose. It was lithe and supple, and the movement was like the movement of a large animal before it springs.

'For God's sake be careful,' shouted Tonia suddenly. 'D'you want to drive into him?' Again it was unlike her to be so on edge, but we slowed right down and Wally Parr took a last photograph of *Bluebird* as Campbell accelerated and the blue car leapt away into the distance. Campbell was taking his greatest risk so far, and we sat in silence watching and wondering how it would end.

Certainly *Bluebird* looked fast enough, although it is always difficult to judge speed at these levels, and there was still that ominous comet tail of yellow behind the car which had always meant before that the track was disintegrating. When *Bluebird* had disappeared over the horizon, we went off in pursuit, following her to the eastern end of the track.

'What was the speed?' Parr asked Norris.

'Around two-fifty.'

'That's all?'

'Track again. He says there was trouble around the second mile mark. We're going up in a minute to look.' As an engineer, Norris has learned to treat disaster discreetly. He has an almost unnatural patience. The only sign of disappointment he would permit himself was to smile ruefully towards the car.

'So you won't have got the recorder readings you need from today's run?' said Parr.

'No.' He drew the word out as if even a simple negative might be committing him to some unintentional inaccuracy. 'Not yet, but let's wait and see what happens.' He walked away, scratching his small moustache.

The inspection team was away nearly half an hour, and when they returned Villa and Norris looked particularly grim. Mustard had his sunglasses on again. Campbell did the talking.

'We seem to have torn up the surface even worse than I feared, and since this track is our lifeline we're not going to risk chopping it up now any more than we have to. So we intend to have one more run this morning and then we will leave the track for four or five days in the hope that the salt hardens and the ruts we've made will heal.'

All this was said quite matter-of-factly as if destroying the optimism and excitement with which the morning had begun was no concern of his. And *Bluebird* set off on the last run of the day.

This time it was fast, undeniably fast, and by the time Tonia reached him at the western end of the track he was out of the cockpit and shouted 'Two ninety-five, darling.' He smiled at her and she kissed him and said, 'Well done, darling,' and everyone was happy again.

And it *was* well done. He had almost achieved what he said he would. He had got the engineers the speed they required for their readings. And later that day news of this run of 'practically 300 mph' made the late editions of the evening papers in Adelaide. After all, as the news stories pointed out, it was the fastest a car had ever been driven in Australia.

Campbell shrugged aside the congratulations of the people who crowded round him. He stood talking to Leo Villa for a while, serious-faced, sucking an empty Dunhill and watching as the little red compressor was started to drive the high-pressure water jet used for hosing away the salt from the car.

Then, more self-contained than ever, he was aboard his aircraft and circling away from the lake back to Muloorina.

No one else was in any hurry to get back to Muloorina. There were sandwiches in the hangar for anyone who wanted them and then one by one, the cars and Land Rovers began to trail off like late guests from a party that had gone on too long.

I drove back with Parr sometime after three. I think we exchanged no more than a dozen words during the whole journey, and as we approached Muloorina and saw the wind-pump and the flat silver triangle of the homestead roof far out across the ochre-coloured plain, a hot wind came up bringing flies and the pale grey dust into the cab of our truck.

Suddenly this dead, lost countryside seemed horribly appropriate for the drama we were involved in. It was all of a piece—the river that led nowhere, the hollow cry of the birds as we crossed the creek, the tin cans, bottles, sheep bones, packing cases half buried in the sand between the saltbushes and the outhouses. When the kangaroos were shot they were slung out here in the morning for the dogs to eat. And when lorries or pumps broke down for the last time, they were abandoned here too, so that the land around the homestead was like a great dry cemetery littered with the remains of ancient trucks, car chassis, boilers, diesel engines, saloon cars. *Bluebird* may have cost more than all of them put together, but it would find a resting-place here as comfortable as the rest.

'Well,' said Parr, as he stopped the engine outside the homestead and lowered himself cautiously out of the cab, 'something's got to happen, but I can't see what.'

Just before seven the sun set and the wind died. The temperature began to fall abruptly and people became more tolerable. One by one they gathered in the kitchen of the homestead for a drink. This had started only during the last few days, but already it was one of the immutable traditions of the place. There was no sign of Campbell although he always provided the drink.

Elliot Price was standing, warming his behind against the kitchen range. He was wearing his boots, his braces and his grey felt hat. He beamed at us as we came in.

'Your man's winning now. Have a real drink and enjoy yourself,' he said.

'It's a bit early to start celebrating, Elliot,' answered Norris.

'It's never too early to celebrate. But what's the matter?'

'What do you think? It's still this lake of yours, Elliot. It's no good. The adhesion's too low, far too low.'

'Well,' said Elliot, scratching himself.

'You see, if *Bluebird* was a jet car like Breedlove's there'd be none of this trouble. The surface of the salt would only have to carry the weight of the car. All the thrust would be generated by the exhaust gases, and the car would literally blow itself along.'

Like most consistently silent men, Norris carries unusual authority when he does speak. He is not a man to argue with. He describes facts because facts are what concern him. And if someone had their facts wrong he had a simple duty to put them right.

'*Bluebird* is a car which drives through the wheels, and because of this its thrust is dependent on the extent its wheels can grip the salt. Now if you're on a flat, hard, dry surface such as concrete, you get an adhesion factor of point eight to point nine and you're safe. As you accelerate the wheels slip minimally and you have the thrust you need. But the less adhesion you have—the less grip—the more danger there is that when you accelerate your wheels will spin like the wheels of a steam engine on wet rails. That's when you lose your thrust and worse still, if you're at any speed, that's when you lose control.'

'And what sort of adhesion factor did you find today?' someone asked.

'That's what worries us,' said Norris, rubbing his nose. 'It varies so much. On that first stretch of track by the eastern end it was showing around point seven. That's not really good, but it's acceptable. From about the third mile mark it falls right off.'

He paused and looked at the rest of us.

'Perhaps it'll improve,' he said. 'I hope so.'

All the time he had been talking, Leo Villa was nodding, saying nothing. His whisky was still in his glass. And when Norris had finished no one spoke. There was an uncomfortable silence. The only sound was the slow hiss of two kettles boiling on the stove.

'Still, Ken,' said Elliot at last, 'he's done three hundred. You can't gainsay it. Near as dammit he has. And three hundred's three-quarters way there.' As he spoke he pushed his hat on to the back of his head and sounded like a man trying to retrieve the mood with which the party had started. But Norris was still concerned with facts.

'No, that's where you're wrong, Elliot. It's about half-way there. All the hazards increase in relation to the square of the speed. From now on we need to watch out.'

'What about the suspension, Ken?' asked Villa. 'What do today's readings show?'

'Well, again it's all right at the moment, but the real problem starts *over* 300. The biggest bump we recorded today at the front axle seems to be around 1.8G. G is the force of gravity so that's equivalent to a wallop of around a couple of tons. Well, she'll take that, although she shouldn't have to. But as I say, all these forces increase at the square of the speed. So a force of 2G at two hundred miles an hour will become 8G at four hundred.'

So, in theory, Wednesday 14 May should have been celebrated as Campbell's best day since he arrived in Australia. Instead it was the start of the worst situation any record breaker can find himself in.

For Campbell was no fool. Whatever his shortcomings he knew about record breaking, and at the end of that second run of his he understood as none of the rest of us could, how enormously greater the odds against him were than even he had previously suspected.

All this showed in his face for a fraction of a second when the canopy lifted after the second run and he was in the cockpit and alone. He looked suddenly very old—not angry as I had seen him, nor bitter as he had been after that last useless run on the main track, but old and very shaken. It was the way his mouth went, the way the lines suddenly accentuated themselves down the side of his face, the way he seemed to lose all expression, all his usual resilience. It was only a moment, but in that moment he seemed to understand that he was finally committed now to something his experience told him would almost certainly be fatal.

With a successful run behind him, everyone, his supporters as well as those who disliked him and criticised him, would now expect him to continue on this death track.

7

The Shadow of Utah

During that third week of May the winds began in earnest, great explosions of wind as if the whole dry continent was suddenly on the move. The sky turned sick as the stifling clouds of umber-coloured dust rumbled across the outback, and the same dust would come seeping beneath the flaps of tents and the mouths of sleeping bags and into hair and eyes and shaving soap and between the tufts of toothbrushes. There were another four days to wait while the lake dried out and Campbell's track was being prepared. And it was during these four days that things began to happen as Parr had said they would.

It began quite suddenly, this change of mood, although it had its origins in the layout of the camp—one of the many mistakes which were to dog Campbell during his time at Lake Eyre.

For the camp was in two distinct parts. Campbell, his close friends, family, engineers and retainers lived at the main homestead. Tonia and Leo's wife Joan were there to do the washing and the cooking, and there were chairs and tables and carpets on the floor and a bath with hot water that lasted with luck until around midday and a deep freeze for the beer. Life was crowded but tolerable enough.

But when the army arrived under the arrangement Campbell had made with the Australian government, they decided to pitch their tents on a ridge half a mile to the south, close to Elliot Price's landing-strip. Certainly it was a good defensive position. There was a fine view from the ridge, and the army had set up six large green bell tents and a guard room and a first aid post and a generating unit and a marquee where green cans of Southwark bitter were sold in the evenings at two shillings a time.

At the moment the camp was still nothing like up to full strength. Just before the record attempt more troops would be sent from Adelaide to man the causeway, control the visitors and carry out some of the heavy work involved. Until then the army camp was practically empty and the obvious place to billet anyone for whom there was no room across at the homestead.

There were beds for them there, and army cooks ready to provide hot meals at any hour of the day or night. Army water trailers supplied first-rate field washing facilities, and at the correct regulation distance from the tents—far enough to keep away the flies but not too far to make the journey an ordeal—stood a neat row of twelve well-regulated army latrines, sweet and clean from the barracks store in Adelaide. Up to a dozen men at a time could use them, sharing the view and the pleasure of each other's company.

With all these benefits the army camp naturally became the centre for all the men who worked on the lake. Almost as a matter of course Andrew Mustard had parked his caravan nearby. So had one or two more of his key personnel.

If the record had been won swiftly none of this would have mattered. But now with the dust storms and the wind and this latest delay, people suddenly noticed that Muloorina was split into two camps, one of which had cool beer and aeroplanes and lavatories that flushed, whilst the other had army cooking and canvas and twelve War Department thunder boxes. And during these few days towards the end of May, the men in the army camp were getting tired of it. To them Campbell was increasingly a figure on the homestead verandah, a face at the window of the Aero Commander's cockpit.

When *Bluebird* actually ran, the camp drew together and discomforts were forgotten with the risks Campbell was taking. But he needed to be a hero now to be acceptable. As the delays piled up he turned into the Englishman every Australian secretly resents.

There was hardly any contact now between the two halves of the camp. Campbell never visited the bar in the marquee during the evening, but in his absence his every motive, every action was exhaustively discussed.

Parr had taken to going to the bar in the evenings to hear what was going on and I would often see him there, a silent, slightly aloof figure on the edge of the crowd, drinking sweet Australian sherry and smiling to himself as he listened to the talk around him.

The inside of the tent was decorated with empty green beer tins threaded through strings and hung between the tent poles. There was a trestle table and a cash-box for whoever was serving, and a large oil-drum for the evening's empties.

The oil-drum was already overflowing with empty cans when I arrived there.

'Why are we hanging around here now?' a fat young man in blue dungarees was shouting. The crowd round the table was considerable and it was hard to get a drink. When you got your beer you had to drink it from the can. There was a strong smell of creosote and male sweat, and the noise was overwhelming. But the man in the dungarees had a powerful voice.

'I'll tell you why. It's because bloody Campbell's lost his nerve. Man, you can tell just by looking at him. He's petrified of the bloody car.'

'Well, he drove it, didn't he,' said a voice. 'Yesterday he drove it and he did three hundred.'

'Too right he drove it,' bellowed the blue dungarees. 'Because he had to. Because everyone was pushing him. But three hundred after we've been here nearly a month. What good is that for God's sake? Why didn't he make a third run in that bloody great car of his and push on up to three-fifty? The car'd do it. I tell you he's scared.'

'And what about you?' said a young sergeant from the police. 'I suppose you'd do it if you were in his place.'

'That's not the point,' he said. 'What I'd do is not the point at all. I don't make the money he does. D'you know how much he's made out of this *Bluebird*? Bloody millions just as his old man did before him. I tell you he's boxing clever with his backers. He's not in this business for fun. He's in for money, and he'll just spin it out again as he did last year.'

'But fair goes,' said the sergeant. 'Either he's scared or he's boxing clever, but he can't be both.'

'Why not?' shouted the other man, getting red in the face. 'I don't see why not. I wouldn't put anything past him.'

'No, you've got it wrong. It's not like that at all.' The voice was quiet, restrained, and its very softness made an impressive answer to the other man's bluster. The speaker was a fair-haired, rather solid man who worked for Andrew Mustard on the lake.

'I don't see how you can say he's scared. He got the water record six times and you don't get a scared man doing that. But I think he's sick. I think that Utah crash did more damage than we've heard about. And I think it's left him with a psychological block about really fast speeds. The closer he gets to the speed he crashed at Utah, the more of a nightmare it will be for him.'

I knew how impatient Wally Parr was becoming by now, but when I walked back towards his quarters with him when the meeting was over he was at his most enigmatic.

'The English are supposed to take their pleasures sadly,' he said. 'As an Australian I try to take other people's sadnesses pleasurably. Come and have a drink. I've something to show you.'

As usual he was wearing a hat with a mosquito net. Along with his army boots and surplus denim trousers, this gave him a serious, dedicated air. His room, for which the Australian Associated Press were paying Elliot Price slightly less than if their employee had been staying at Claridges, was in a long, corrugated-iron hut, and was conveniently close to the mobile post office through which he filed his copy to Adelaide. It had a cement floor, a chair, and a large iron bedstead with a prolapsed mattress. And with that obscure ability to make himself comfortable anywhere which is perhaps the surest mark of nature's newspapermen, he had filled it with his personal collection of paperbacks, old socks, shaving equipment, bottles, transistor radios and spare pairs of trousers. His typewriter was on the chair and he had just started reading Mary McCarthy's book *The Group*.

'D'you know,' he said, as he poured three-quarters of an inch of Johnnie Walker for me into his Pepsodent-tasting tooth mug, 'this ridiculous book is actually banned in the worthy state of Victoria, and as a result there's not a housewife in Melbourne who hasn't read it. Australia must be one of the last places in the world where the authorities really give one an incentive to read serious literature.'

'It looks as though you'll have time to get through it, anyhow,' I said.

'I'm not so sure there won't be other things to do. As I said this afternoon, I've a hunch things are just starting to get interesting now. Take this business of the crash at Utah, for instance. I should have thought of it a long time ago, but when I left I paid a call on Ken Norris and asked him about it. He lent me this.'

He rummaged among the litter of papers and magazines on the end of the bed and produced a thin, grey-covered folder. Typed on the front was the title—'Campbell-Norris 7. Land Speed Record Attempt 1960. Report no. 60/18D/RI.'

'I was looking through it before dinner,' he said. 'Take a look yourself, and excuse me if I remove my boots while you're reading. I think page eight is the part that will interest you.'

The report had been run off on a duplicator and the typewritten pages had blurred slightly, although there were perfectly legible. I began to read from it:

Bonneville Salt Flats, Friday 16 September 1960.

Run 5. South to North. Start approx. 6.22 a.m. Wind was gusting 3 to 6 mph from SSE as the car was wound up to 9500 compressor revolutions per minute and D.M.C. pulled away well to the right hand of the central black line to miss the pothole at mile 1. Ambient temperature was down to 17°C, so relatively good engine performance was expected. D.M.C.'s comments at the end of the run were as follows:

a   Speed at the end of three miles—300 mph.
    (K. W. Norris reminded D.M.C. that 300 mph was required in 2 miles for the record.)
b   C.rpm up to 10,000 plus.
c   Stopping procedure. Engine cut—air brakes out, foot brakes on 120-lb/sq. in. at 7½ mile mark—speed down from 260 to 95 mph in 3 miles. Mechanical brakes very good indeed.
d   Jet pipe temperature reached 600°C max.
e   Steering was light and the car wanted to wander off.

In general everyone was very happy with the run…

D.M.C. again requested that during run 6 he should try both the acceleration of the car and also braking hard at the other end.

'It's run number six that's the important one,' said Parr. 'Very strange style these engineers use when they're writing their reports.'

About 1.6 miles (i.e. 1.5 miles from mile 0, there being 0.1 miles from mile 0 to the start of the run) up the course, CN7 (the official abbreviation for the car) started to go off track, finishing nearly broadside on at 1.9 miles in a spiral left-hand slide. From then on the car took off for nearly 200 yards, bouncing several times before coming to rest approximately 500 yards away on the salt to the left of the course and into the wind.

But Ken Norris had obviously thought that the occasion demanded something more than this, and he added the following first-person account:

7.10 a.m. and as CN7 pulled away it was obvious that she was accelerating very fast and Leo and I made a quick dash for our Rover follow-up car which was parked about 20 yards away facing the course. We were quickly up to 90 mph on the right-hand side of the right-hand marker line but CN7 was by then a speck on the horizon. Suddenly there appeared to be more 'dust' than usual surrounding CN7 and then from this cloud a blue object flew upwards. My immediate thought was that the top plenum chamber cover had flown off and I cursed myself inwardly for not doing more stringent tests. My immediate reaction that the Skipper would be okay if it was indeed the top cover, was quickly dispelled as the cloud had now increased considerably and appeared to be way to the left-hand of the course. Leo's comment was 'My God, he's in trouble,' and I prayed, 'Please God he's all right,' as Leo plunged across the track heading straight for the cloud. We were doing a good 90 mph and it took us a mere 60 seconds to reach what was left of the car, but those 60 seconds seemed endless. The past kept imposing itself with endless accusations. You should have done this and that and that!!! I don't remember anything of the wreckage on the way across the salt, my eyes being fixed on the black blob ahead. As we drew near, it seemed that CN7 was upside down and I felt sick and empty inside—but closer still and it was apparent that she was the right way up, and as Leo was screeching to a halt I was preparing to jump from the doorway. I could think of nothing but reaching the canopy and yanking it up. I could see Donald's head nodding to and fro dazedly inside, the crash helmet looking weird and ungainly. Another leap and I yanked the canopy external release at the front end. A jump and I was on the wreck at the back end of the canopy and trying to prise up the perspex. Leo was now at the front and he pulled the release again and the canopy came up easily.

Blood was spattered on places over the Skipper's blue overalls, but he seemed okay otherwise. Consciousness of the engine running sweetly impelled me to action again and I skipped down the far side of the canopy and grabbed across the cockpit for the emergency fuel cut-off. Nothing happened, and Leo and I pulled on the release together. The engine stopped and Peter Carr was leaning over the far side of the cockpit to release the harness. Tonia was running across the salt, her legs dragging slower and slower as she approached. Thumbs up and a short 'he's okay' and she came on again as strong arms were dragging the Skipper free. The ambulance was now alongside, the stretcher was out and Tonia was hovering over the Skipper as he mumbled, 'I seem to have clouted my ear' on the way to the ambulance.

'Go away pressmen, can't you see he's hurt? No, we don't know what's happened yet.'

The ambulance pulled away and we gazed dumbfounded at what a few seconds past was to be the fastest car in the world. Dejection followed as we wandered slowly back through scattered wreckage to the course and the start of the trouble.

I looked across at Parr. Miss McCarthy seemed to be claiming all his attention.

'Finished?' he asked, without taking his eyes from the book.

'Hardly what you'd expect from our friend Norris, is it?' he said.

The hall was tiny and packed with an obscure smell of dust and good works, and Tonia sang for over an hour. There was no stage in the mission hall at Marree but that hardly worried her, and she sang before her audience of storekeepers and sheepmen's wives as if her life depended on it. She was a great success. The applause was enthusiastic.

She had agreed to give this performance to raise funds for the mission in the local Aborigine settlement, and when she sang it was uncanny the way she suddenly turned into a person none of us had seen at Lake Eyre. The illusion was total. She could have been in Paris or Las Vegas, and she sang as if she was proving to herself that there was a world which existed outside the nightmare of Lake Eyre. She could still make an audience respond as she had done so many times before, still be the controlled professional self which all her training had made her.

Marree is the nearest thing to *High Noon* to be found these days outside the Middle West, and as we came from the hall we passed the Aborigine cattle men strolling through the late afternoon dust in their high-heeled boots on the way from the stockyard, and saw the small neat clapboard houses and the tethering posts for the horses along the main street. And before driving back to Muloorina we had a drink at the Bar Marree (Konstantinos Sideris, Licensed Dealer in Wines and Spirits). It was a long, bleak, unlovely room with shining apple-green walls and a lino-covered bar and fluorescent lighting on the ceiling and a large black notice beside the advertisements for Craven Filter saying, 'If you have not reached the age of twenty-one please do not order liquor as the penalty is severe.'

Tonia was happy and relaxed after her performance, and the strain which had begun to show during the last few days at Muloorina had vanished entirely. She was smiling now and her face was very sunburned.

'I had almost forgotten how much I need to work,' she said. 'It's bad for me if I don't sing. My career is really as important to me as Donald's is to him, and when this is over I'll be picking it up again. I've a recording contract in Paris and then a lot of work in New York. You know,' she said, 'Donald used to be very jealous of my work and when I married him I gave it all up. There was a part in a musical on Broadway and a film with David Niven too. They both went. It was a great mistake. You see, no woman can stand the strain of all this unless she has another life as well. His first two wives couldn't take it. One of the reasons I can is that I've got my career back again now, and when all this is over I'll just go off on tour and sing.'

Lake Eyre could have been a whole continent away.

'The secret of my marriage with Donald,' she went on, 'is not to be demanding. The more demanding a woman becomes the more elusive he is, and if I ever became an ordinary housewife he'd get bored and that would be that.'

'That's hardly likely,' I said.

She nodded but did not smile. 'No, you're right there.'

She was silent then and stood sipping her lemonade and watching the beginning of a fight at the far end of the bar among some men from the railway.

Donald Campbell with *Bluebird*
before the Utah crash.

Donald preparing for a test run
on Lake Eyre in May 1963.

Tonia and Donald in 1958.

Donald (centre) confers with Ken Norris, co-designer of *Bluebird*, and Andrew Mustard, who has just checked the condition of the track in his Elfin racing car.

Donald and his team pushing *Bluebird* back into its shelter at sunset.

Mechanics checking *Bluebird*'s huge wheels and
tyres, which had to be removed and re-balanced after each run.

On the eve of his record breaking run, Donald surveys the blue line marked on the salt which he followed to establish his World Land Speed Record.

JEFF CARTER

'Now, boys. Now, *now*, boys,' shouted the barman. 'Just cut it out, boys. I'm not losing me licence because of you. Now cut it out.' He was a small hairless man with an impressive voice, and order was restored.

'We're different from other people,' she said at last. 'That's the truth of it. Donald's not like an ordinary husband and I'm not like any ordinary wife. We're restless, crazy, obsessed sort of people. At times it's hell and at times it's wonderful.

'Look at Donald now. D'you think I enjoy being with him and watching him at a time like this? D'you think I don't want to tell him twenty times a day to get out of Lake Eyre and forget it and settle down somewhere and start enjoying life again? But winning this record is part of him. He's got to do it and no one will stop him.

'Perhaps you think I don't know the danger he's in. Believe me, I know it. I live every minute of it when he's in that car. But it's something he has to go through and I have to go through it with him. You know Donald,' she said. 'Can you imagine what he'd be like for the rest of his life if he left Lake Eyre now?

'I saw an old newsreel,' she went on. 'A very old one of Donald as a small boy greeting his father on his return from Daytona with a new record. It was the time Sir Malcolm got his knighthood I think. And this picture of Donald was one of the saddest things I've ever seen. There he was, this very English schoolboy on the quay at Southampton—his hair brushed, his best suit on, excited out of his life. Then there was a shot of Sir Malcolm coming down the gang-plank—smiling, successful, surrounded by admirers and reporters—a real hero, and my poor Donald never got a look in. You could see him on the edge of the crowd trying to catch his father's attention, desperately trying to reach him, but never quite managing it.

'I think Donald is still that small boy,' she said. 'And now his ambition ruins most of the things that make a normal man happy. If he gave up now he would never forgive himself—or me.'

Campbell lowered himself carefully into an old blue and white deckchair and began filling his pipe from a pigskin tobacco pouch.

'Have they got round to saying yet that I've lost my nerve?'

'Yes.'

'There's always someone says that if you get held up on a record bid longer than a week or two. In 1955 we were held up nearly six months at Ullswater trying to persuade the hydroplane to go through the water barrier. You should have heard what one or two uncharitable people called me then.'

He settled himself comfortably, got his feet on to a box of tinned peas, then turned his attention to persuading his pipe alight. 'But what are they saying now?'

'A lot of loose talk. You don't have to take any notice of it.'

'No, I want to know.' The pale eyes were watching me closely through the clouds of fresh smoke.

I told him. 'They're saying that the Utah crash has left you with a sort of phobia about really high speeds and that you'll never risk approaching the same speed again.'

'Ah,' he said, nodding. 'So that's it.'

He was silent for a while still sucking away at his pipe. Then he shifted and looked at me again.

'D'you want to know what really happened?' he said.

'Only if you want to tell me.'

'It was a strange business—a very strange business, believe you me. You see, when I took *Bluebird* out to Bonneville in 1960 I went convinced that I was going to kill myself. I had a presentiment of death when I was on holiday in Majorca just before I started the trip. It's the one time in my life I've had it, and sure enough everything went wrong from then on.'

'I remember it all so well. At the start of that second run I had felt almost light-headed with excitement, totally without fear. I gave *Bluebird* all she'd got and saw the speedo reading three twenty, three hundred and twenty mark you, as the *first* mile marker flashed past.'

'Jolly good, I said to myself, old Ken will be pleased. But then,

then, instead of slackening off and going back very pleased with myself as I had every right to be, I put my foot down harder still. Madness.'

He thumped his knee and paused a moment, glaring into space. 'Sheer flaming bloody madness.

'I knew she was going out of control. Felt it. Actually felt the tail slipping. And I knew what would happen. I knew we'd crash but none of it seemed to concern me. I just sat there in that split second thinking "well, this is the end," and not feeling the remotest interest.

'The rest, you know. The car took off, shot nearly a thousand yards, miraculously staying the right way up, and bumped six times on the deck before coming to a standstill. When Ken and old Leo opened up the canopy I was unconscious of course—covered in blood. I'd had one hell of a crack on the head, but I was alive and I came to in the ambulance.

'The first thing I remember after the crash was seeing Tonia, bless her heart, peering through the window at me from the front of the ambulance, and hearing old Peter Carr my project manager saying, "Wave to her, Don. She's worried stiff. Wave to her and show her you're all right."

'So I waved and did my best to smile and said, "Tell her the jolly old family jewels are still intact." And at the hospital, when the tried carting me in on a stretcher I said, "Not on your sweet life. The Bluebird Project's not ending with a picture in all the evening papers of yours truly on a stretcher." So I held on to old Peter and just managed to make it through the hospital door on my own pins.

'But why had it happened? What had made me behave like that?'

He stopped and looked at me as if I ought to know the answer for myself. 'Oxygen,' he said finally. 'The oxygen I'd been breathing at the time of the crash. On the advice of several experts we had fitted an oxygen breathing system to the car and, as we discovered much later, there are certain people—and of course I had to be one of them—who experience a form of drunkenness if they inhale pure oxygen at sea level.

'It was as simple as that. I had been inhaling pure oxygen throughout the two runs and all the symptoms fitted in with those we found in reports of experiments on combat pilots during the war—elation, loss of all sense of fear and reality, slowing down of reaction—the whole works. They call it oxygen poisoning.'

'But what about the effect the crash had on you—the nervous trouble. How bad was that?'

'Old boy, it was something I wouldn't wish on my worst enemy. It was terrifying. If I hadn't lived through it, I would never have believed it possible.'

He paused, discovered his pipe was out, and leaned forward to relight it.

'When they got me inside that hospital they seemed to think at first there was nothing much the matter with me apart from cuts and severe shock and concussion. They X-rayed me, but the real damage to the skull didn't show up. It was only when cerebral spinal fluid started trickling out of my ear that one of the doctors said, "Hey, this man has fractured the base of his skull. He's lucky to be alive at all."

'It took a long time to get over. A very long time, believe you me. For several months after the crash I was like a very old man, terrified of anything out of the ordinary. I couldn't so much as drive a car. I didn't want to meet people. It was agony for me to make any decision. All I could do was to stay at home, and the only real relief was in bed.

'Then it began to lift. I didn't look quite so ghastly and I was able to get on a bit with the business of rebuilding *Bluebird* and starting up the whole project again.'

'But you never had any doubts about wanting another go at the record?' I asked.

He seemed surprised. 'Doubts, old boy? No, why? The only thing to do was to go on. But I can tell you it was no easy matter getting a new car built. The old one was a complete write-off.

During 1961 and 1962 there were some fairly frantic periods of overwork, and that was when I found the nervous attacks recurring. They'd take the form of unimaginable fear. Totally and utterly without reason. I'd just be certain suddenly that I was going to die.'

'And when did you have the last attack?'

'Oh, a long time ago. This brain business tends to right itself with time if you're lucky. I've been lucky.'

May's last week began, and the trouble which had been getting closer and closer to the deceptively quiet surface of life at Muloorina came bubbling up. It began on Monday evening. The telephone in the sitting room started ringing, and there was a journalist from Sydney on the line asking for Campbell.

'There's a report in a London paper that because of the delays and the trouble you've run into, your most important backers are pulling out, Mr Campbell. Have you any comment you would like to make at this stage?'

'Totally and completely untrue,' replied Campbell. 'I said, sir, that the report is totally and completely untrue. Your source of information is seriously misinformed.'

There was a pause. 'I said it's rubbish, sir. I have no backers so I fail to see how they could have pulled out. If they are referring to the association I had with the British Petroleum Company, that ended by mutual consent nearly six months ago. I am financing this attempt out of my own pocket. Good-night to you, sir.'

He replaced the telephone carefully and stayed sitting in the armchair for some while without speaking to anyone.

This meant real trouble now. Denials were no use with a story like this, although everything he had said on the telephone was true. He had no backers in the normal sense of the term, no sympathetic financiers or industrialists supplying him with money which could be suddenly cut off as the Sydney reporter had suggested. His long association with BP (under which the oil company had pumped its estimated quarter of a million pounds into the Bluebird

Project in return for the right to exploit Campbell and any records he won for advertising purposes) had ended in December 1963 when Campbell had rejected BP's proposal to put their own manager in charge of the Bluebird Project and pay Campbell all his expenses plus a handsome bonus on attaining the record.

'You can only have one man in charge of an operation like this,' Campbell had said at the time. 'I've never heard of a record yet that was won by a committee.'

His subsequent agreement with Ampol was a straightforward deal under which the Australian oil company supplied him with his fuel and oil and paid a lump sum for the right to advertise the fact that they were doing so. The same again was promised if he got the record. And all the rest of the money he had been promised from outside sources depended now on the record. And if he failed?

'If I fail this time, old scout,' he had said in a moment of candour, 'I shall be a very poor man.'

He must have been thinking of this later that night when he called an unexpected meeting up at the army camp, 'just to put the record straight'. For mysteriously the news about backers pulling out had already got around the entire camp. Nobody quite new what it meant but the phrase sounded convincing and by now many people were ready to believe that the attempt was about to fold.

There was a touch of desperation about the way he spoke. He was wearing a new dark-blue quilted nylon anorak he had ordered from a store in Adelaide.

'I would like to tell you all that some misinformed individuals have been spreading totally false information about the Bluebird Project and saying that certain "backers" are withdrawing their support. I don't know, gentlemen, where this information has come from, but I would like to state here and now that it is totally and completely incorrect.'

He paused to look at the ring of faces surrounding him. Mustard and Dibben were in the front row. Parr was to the left, and Superintendent Brebner was standing by the entrance to the tent, his gaunt sad face overtopping the crowd in front. But there was no reaction from anyone, and Campbell continued in the silence.

'Whatever difficulties we have had to encounter, gentlemen, I still intend to go forward towards the record slowly, determinedly, scientifically.'

He shifted now and stood facing us sternly. 'No record, gentlemen, has ever been won without a struggle.'

But struggles alone were not enough that week. Despite all Campbell's denials, several Sydney papers appeared next morning with two-inch front-page headlines announcing that his backers *were* pulling out. And when he tried a run with *Bluebird* on the Tuesday morning on the new track—the final one—which Mustard's men had now completed, he complained that it was 'like driving over old bricks,' and his top speed was two hundred and fifty miles an hour.

Campbell slept most of that afternoon, and appeared in the sitting room in search of a drink around 5.30. He looked rested and assured.

'I've been thinking about the old man,' he said, 'and wondering what he would have done in my place. He probably wouldn't have put up with this present caper for one moment. He wouldn't have stayed being buggered about by Lake Eyre. He'd have been out of here like a dose of salts. But you see, old scout, I've got to stay now. Things are rather different for me.'

He leaned against the mantelpiece by one of the vases of plastic lilac and carefully poured himself a vodka and tonic—half an inch of vodka, the rest tonic.

'He was without question the greatest man I've ever known. He was the best at this game, and no one's ever equalled him. He could be very formidable when he wanted to, my father. Very, very formidable.'

He sipped his drink, then held the glass up to inspect it.

'I don't drink much these days, you know. The old tum's not really up to wine or beer any more. Old age, I suppose. Catches up with you in many ways. The reactions begin to slow down a bit although you make up for that in experience if you're sensible. That's what Father did—used his sense and his experience and cut down the element of chance. He was built to last. You know he was fifty-four in 1939 when he got his last record, and if it hadn't been for the war he'd have carried on longer still.

'I've asked Andrew Mustard and all his boys in for a drink before dinner,' he said casually. 'If we're going to get the record now, that track's got to be smoother and they're the only people who can do it.'

Just then Andrew Mustard arrived. He looked shy and unwell.

'Good evening, Mr Mustard,' said Campbell, 'and good evening, gentlemen,' he said as the rest of Mustard's team filed into the room. It was the first time they had been to the homestead for a drink like this and some of them had put on ties for the occasion.

When everyone was seated the Johnnie Walker was passed silently round. There was the muffled crack and hiss of beer cans opening, and people shuffled uneasily in their seats wondering exactly what Campbell was up to now. He looked carefully at all those faces before he spoke.

'Gentlemen, we're up against it.' He was earnest, a little unsure of himself. 'The car can do it. I believe *I* can do it. But on top of that we need a miracle and it is a miracle that only you gentlemen can perform. I have got to gamble on your ability to get the salt of the new track as smooth for its whole length as it is for the first three miles.

'Now I know this is asking the impossible of you, but believe me, we need the impossible. And if it makes you feel any happier, I'm prepared to put five hundred pounds in the kitty to be shared among you.'

He paused and lit his pipe. If he was expecting any reaction to his offer, none came. No one moved. I watched Andrew Mustard. He was sitting on the sofa, and the line of china geese on the wall behind him looked as if they were flying out of his head. The lilac on the mantelpiece seemed to have grown.

Campbell stood and waited for a reply and the silence lengthened. It was one of those crucial moments when people's opinions are in the balance and almost anything can be said.

Someone cleared his throat. More eyes were turned towards Andrew Mustard and for a moment it seemed as if he was going to speak.

Instead, by yet another minor freak of circumstance, the large mahogany chiming clock which was the pride of the Prices' mantelpiece chose this moment to strike seven and the moment was lost. Instead of the criticism and the anxiety coming out then and being dealt with, point by point, as it still might have been, it stayed where it was. Stan Dibben said something about the need for the greatest urgency in going for the record once the work on the track was finished. Campbell said, of course no one was more aware of the need for urgency than he was.

That was that, and Campbell seemed to think he had won. As the Johnnie Walker began its second journey, he began speaking again and his voice was steadier, more confident than before. He insisted now on the need for fifteen clear runs in *Bluebird* so that the engineers would have a chance to test and adjust the car all the way up to the record.

'Give me those runs, gentlemen, on a track like a billiard table and I will promise you the record. Some people have been saying I should put my foot down right now and get the record that way. But believe me, that's not the way. That's the way to smash the car and probably the pilot too. I tried it once at Utah four years ago when I was drunk on oxygen. I'm not doing it again.'

It was an impressive speech.

'One last thing, gentlemen. It is now Tuesday. This weekend I'm getting the timekeepers up. I will not run on that track until you tell me it's ready. But as soon as you do, you will have the satisfaction of knowing that every run I make over three hundred will be timed officially. And I would like to remind you that in this game we don't make records. We make timed trials over measured distances.'

That night the dogs that slept outside the homestead were kept awake until after midnight by the noise of hammering and a weird blue light sputtering from one of the outbuildings. Tom Scrimshire was welding a pair of new drags for smoothing the track, and before dawn they were on their way to the lake.

The rain that was forecast passed to the east and then down to Port Augusta and Adelaide, and by Friday night Mustard reported that the track was nearly ready. It was hard and smooth for something over eleven miles. The worst point lay where it crossed the old track at the south end but there was hope that even this could be improved.

It was on Friday too that the first of the timekeepers arrived. They spent Saturday on the lake with the official surveyor, measuring Campbell's mile to the nearest half-inch, and setting up tripods for the cameras which were synchronised with an electronic clock to measure the car's entrance and exit through the mile to a thousandth of a second.

Official stewards were still needed before Campbell could set a new record, but they were due to arrive any time now. On Saturday evening Campbell announced that he would be making his first timed run early the following morning.

'Perhaps I was wrong,' said Parr that night. 'Perhaps he's really got a chance after all.'

8

Vibrations

On the last Sunday in May he rose just after six, breakfasted on toast and coffee, and decided to drive the Morris 1100 to the lake himself. He was calm. He was silent. And as he drove the Morris with such assurance through the dust, the morning haze, across the flat dry countryside to Lake Eyre, he looked ready at last to do what he had to do. The sun had risen. The salt glittered gold and pink and his task seemed suddenly very simple. He would drive the car, he would get what he wanted, and none of the criticisms, none of the doubts, none of the memories of childhood and fears of middle age would matter any longer.

We rumbled along the battered road to the causeway, slowed down to pass through the checkpoint the army was manning to keep unauthorised visitors from the lake.

'Good luck,' shouted the military police sergeant as he waved us through. 'Good luck,' shouted the corporal in the large wide-awake hat.

'Why the hell do they have to say that,' muttered Campbell under his breath. 'It's always unlucky.' And he went on to tell how the old waterman at Lake Coniston had said 'good luck' to him just before he drove his boat in 1951 and hit the submerged log at one hundred and eighty. 'He'd never said good luck to me before, and afterwards I asked him why he did then. He said he never knew.'

At the base camp there was a new atmosphere. *Bluebird* was already out of the hangar and ready to run, and everyone seemed to have a measure of goodwill for Campbell.

Mustard had been buzzing up and down the track in his red torpedo of a racing car to test the surface. The timekeeper's photo-electric apparatus was between the seventh and eighth mile mark.

'Everything's ready, Donald,' said Mustard, wiping salt from his beard and smiling his faint smile. 'You'll never get the track any better than it is today. She's hard and she's smooth.'

Campbell nodded and said nothing.

'Okay, Skipper?' asked Villa, bustling forward. 'Everything okay. It looks a good day for a run.'

And it did. It seemed as if after all the false starts Lake Eyre was going to play straight with Campbell and at last allow him to try for his record on even terms.

Everything went smoothly, and Campbell was in the cockpit, just completing his check through, when a fault was discovered in one of the brake callipers for the front wheel. It was not serious. Normally it would have taken half an hour to change, but through an oversight the only spare was back at Muloorina, and it was eleven o'clock before the spare had been collected, fitted, tested, and the car was ready to run again.

It was the wrong time to have a delay. Campbell had two and a half hours to worry about the military policeman who had wished him luck and the boatman who had done the same thirteen years earlier at Coniston. Mustard had two and a half hours to worry about the surface of the new track. 'In this heat, Donald, I suggest we should specifically ban any runs after midday. Already you will find it considerably softer than it was at eight.'

Worst of all, the mood changed. We drank coffee. We waited. Campbell signed a few autographs for visitors and chatted to Tonia and watched the engineers as they worked away, stripping down the front wheel assembly. By the time he was back in the cockpit and ready to move off again, the promise had gone from the day.

For the first run, Campbell chose the north end. This gave several of us a chance to wait by the measured mile to see him pass. We had the Morris 1100 again. Wally Parr was with us, wearing very large sunglasses with gold rims. The combination of these with the mosquito net on his hat was disturbing. Tonia was with us too, huddled into the back seat, looking tense and white-faced as she tried to hold Campbell's boots and Whacko the teddy bear and keep her fingers crossed all at the same time. She was wearing a red, white and blue striped shirt and blue silk slacks. Her hair was tied, with white ribbon, and she looked pretty and out of her element, as if she had finally given up trying to understand why her husband had to be here, risking his life at such a time and in such a place and under such conditions.

The control radio the Morris carried began its pedantic squawking from the front seat, as the track controller at the north end of the course told the timekeepers to get ready.

'Mobile One to timekeepers. The torch is alight. *Bluebird* is rolling.' And we waited, straining our eyes to that strange horizon where the mirages danced above the salt islands, and the only landmarks were the spider's web lattice of the film towers and the yellow cubes of the mile markers along the track. We waited for the small black dot to appear, a dot that would come skimming towards us out of nothingness and only at the last moment metamorphose itself into the blue snout, fish tail, haunched wheel fairings of the car, before speeding away down the measured mile, past the tripod legs of the timekeepers' apparatus, trailing its thin yellow tail of salt. It was very beautiful. It was very exciting. It silenced all doubts, answered all criticisms.

No one in the car said anything, and before Campbell was past we had started the engine and raced away to be there as soon as he opened the cockpit.

When we got to *Bluebird* she was resting alone. It was the first time I had seen the car stationary on the salt without something

near it, and it looked unearthly in the middle of such emptiness—
the only object, the only sign of life—and as the cockpit lid rose it
was like watching the first movement from a rocket that had
landed on a new planet.

But when we ran over and peered in at him as he sat there with
his silver crash helmet still on, he wore an expression I had seen
several times before.

'Well, we are in dire trouble,' he said, without looking at any of
us. He lifted off his helmet, handed it to Tonia still without speaking directly to anyone. His voice had a resigned impersonal note to
it, as if he were reporting something that had nothing particularly
to do with him.

'At three-twenty, just before the measured mile, I got high-
frequency vibrations so badly that I could hardly see, let alone steer
properly. It was as much as I could do to hang on to the wheel, and
the whole car was bumping so hard that the track was a blur.'

Disaster seemed to call out a particular eloquence in him, and
the cameras around him began to click, making immortal his
despair on squares of coloured celluloid. From the Morris came the
sound of the radio as it clacked the queries of the checkpoints across
the lonely ether. 'Mobile Two to Project One. What are further
intentions? Please inform additional movements. Over.'

Campbell had heaved himself on to the back of the cockpit and
lit a cigarette. He smoked grimly, as if drawing a bitter wisdom from
the tobacco. He continued his impersonal narrative of disaster.

'There was some discrepancy between the Air Speed Indicator
and the speedometer on the dashboard, but I estimate *Bluebird* was
doing something just over three ten when the vibrations started.
The vibrations themselves were at around three hundred cycles a
second. I cut power at once and eased her down. There was nothing
else to be done. The frequency was so great that at first I thought
something must be broken. It was like nothing I've experienced
before except in the boat at very high speed.'

He finished his cigarette and no one spoke. I saw Andrew
Mustard looking at him intently, but he said nothing.

'It felt as if the wheels could be out of balance, Ken,' he said.

But Andrew Mustard assured Norris that all the wheels had been accurately balanced before the run. Campbell repeated the question, but Mustard shook his head.

Other possibilities for the vibrations were gloomily considered. Norris scratched his chin with his pencil and began calculations on his pad to se if they could be explained by the twisting of the half shaft and there was talk of possible trouble with the suspension. Finally it was decided to reduce tyre pressures from 145 to 125 pounds per square inch. At least it was action of a sort.

It was the most hopeless moment of the whole attempt, for by now we were all involved. We had waited so long and been so drawn into his hopes and his difficulties and his disappointments, that it was our failure as well as his. The big army wrecker truck drew up, and the REME men manning it looked like troops after a surrender. One of them, but only one, lit a cigarette. The skull and horns of a large buffalo had been attached to the radiator, and in that bright sunlight the skull seemed to grin at the long useless shape of the blue car.

'How fast did you say, Donald?' asked Evan Green, the project manager, a good-looking conciliatory man who held the record for driving all round Australia. 'Three-twenty?'

'Well, old chum, there was this ten-mile discrepancy between the two instruments.'

'Still, Donald, whichever it is, you have just driven *Bluebird* faster than any vehicle has ever been driven in Australia before.'

I walked away from the car. It was one-twenty in the afternoon. The sun was very hot, the salt bright gold. The cars in the distance seemed to drown in the mirage as if in water. Men turned into black insects clambering across the glare.

Wally Parr joined me and we strolled over to one of the trucks where he had left a thermos of tea.

Pat Crowe was there, the solid young photographer from the *Adelaide Advertiser* who looks like the last King of Romania on the stamps they issued before he was deposed.

'What Campbell needs,' said Parr, 'is not another car or another track, but a good psychoanalyst.' We nodded. It was probably unjust, but it relieved our feelings.

'But if he really did feel the vibrations,' said Crowe slowly, 'I can't say I blame him. If it happened to me at three hundred miles an hour, I know damn well I'd chop the power.'

Parr's thermos had a fawn lid which unscrewed to form two cups. He filled one and handed it to me.

'But that's just the point,' said Parr. 'You and I are not doing it. We've not been paid to do it. He has. It's his bloody responsibility. All these years he has been getting his name in the papers. Now he's got to deliver. And you know why he's been getting his name in the papers. Just because he's supposed *not* to be like the rest of us. A real record breaker can't allow himself the reactions of an ordinary man. This was his chance to prove all his critics wrong, and he's bungled it.'

He poured himself some tea. It was the first time I had seen him angry. He took off his hat and his sunglasses and glared at *Bluebird* in the distance.

'But what you're asking is that the man should be willing to kill himself,' said Pat Crowe. 'That's too much. You can't ask any man to do that.'

'That's his job. That's always been the job of these record break-ers. They all had to be willing to kill themselves, otherwise there wouldn't have been any records. D'you think Cobb would have chopped power just now? D'you think his father would?'

Bluebird was still sitting where she had rested—elegant, ludicrous, unloved. Small men in white overalls bustled round her.

'I'm sure that every time they set a record, they did so by going just that bit beyond what they thought a man could survive. That's why they were famous, and that's why there were records. And that's what this man won't do. And that's why he's not a record breaker and why we might as well all go home.'

He finished his tea, threw away the dregs from the cup on the salt, and carefully replaced his hat.

'So you want it to be a blood sport,' I said.

'Of course I do. Record breaking must be a blood sport, otherwise it's not record breaking and there's no point to it. If there's no risk to the damned driver anyone could get a record simply by paying a million or so for a new car, and if that's all it is, you might as well spend your million on sound test equipment and set up your record in the laboratory. You'll learn a lot more that way.'

The technicians had finished by now. The sandwiches of cheese, corned beef and lettuce had been bolted down, and Campbell had announced that, late as it was, he would try one more run to test out the release mechanism for the safety parachute.

We went to the Morris 1100, and waited once again to see if the run would be any different this time. But it was slower, and when we reached *Bluebird* at the end of the track we found that he had applied brakes, air-brakes and parachute.

This time nobody asked questions and nobody bothered to take pictures. Tom Scrimshire had toothache, and began gloomily winding up the parachute from where it had trailed behind the car.

Later than usual, Leo Villa came puffing up, looking solider, loyaler than ever.

'Everything okay, Skipper, that time?' he called out.

'Pretty rough, Unc. Pretty rough.'

'That's the lot then for today, Skipper?'

'That's the lot now, Unc. I'll drive her down the course under her own power and then back to base.'

As we followed him back to the base camp, the whole nature of what we were all up to suddenly became clear. It was not a record bid we were watching. It was not just a motor car which was trying to go faster than any motor car had ever gone before. We were watching the trial of a man. The car, the wind, the surface of the lake, were merely instruments on which to test him like the hazards of medieval justice when a man was put to the test. And as with those cruel, illogical trials of the past, the truth we were trying to find out was some inner truth of his character, and the lake and the car between them were our only means of knowing.

Had he lost his nerve? Was there some fear which held him back? Did he really want to go through with the attempt, or was there something from his past making it impossible for him ever to achieve this record he had suffered so much for already?

At the camp the trial was adjourned as the car was jacked up and hosed and wheeled back to the brown creosote-smelling hangar for another night, and Campbell took a car back to Muloorina with his wife. She drove. He slept almost all the way.

There was a fug of tobacco, an air of bitterness and disbelief and tension in the marquee at the army camp when the meeting was held that night to discuss the latest hold-up to the program. The lighting was very bright. Benches had been set in a horseshoe around the trestle table where Campbell was sitting alone in the glare of the hundred-and-fifty-watt bulbs that had been strung just above his head between the tent poles. He looked paler than usual. He tried lighting a cigarette but his lighter would not work, and when no one seemed to notice or offer him a light he slipped the cigarette back into the packet.

The lighting and the close-packed benches and the silence that fell the moment Campbell had entered marked this meeting off immediately from all the other interminable get-togethers and press conferences preceding it. For most of the other meetings had been held to provide something for us to do, and to reassure us that things were happening and that we were not left out. Tonight's meeting was different.

It looked like a field tribunal improvised to get the truth in a hurry, and from the moment he spoke Campbell had reacted awkwardly to it, speaking anxiously, a shade too loudly, as he usually did at the prospect of criticism he could not cope with.

The strangest thing about the meeting was the silence. Perhaps there were people there who believed Campbell really had felt the vibrations. Norris probably did. He was sitting to his left, looking tired and worried and holding a file of papers which he never opened. Leo Villa would have believed him too, for belief in Campbell was part of his life.

But apart from them there can have been no one that night who did not have his doubts.

'Well, gentlemen, I'm pretty confident about what happened this afternoon,' began Campbell with sad jauntiness. 'The suspension is inoperative. The precise cause has yet to be discovered, but I suspect the injection of emulsified salt at high speeds.'

He paused as if waiting to be challenged, but no one spoke. The moment affected Mustard more than anyone else in the room. If Campbell really was cracking now, if these vibrations of his were only one more delayed symptom of his brain injury, it would be Mustard's turn to take over. As reserve driver he would have to drive *Bluebird* and show that he at least had the courage to get the record. He, not Campbell, might become holder of the world land speed record.

But it was a difficult position for him that night. It was one thing to suspect that Campbell was suffering from nervous hallucinations. It was another to prove it so conclusively that Campbell, most jealous and obstinate of men, would give up this car he had worked ten years to complete. And Mustard kept silent as Campbell continued.

'We think that the terrible conditions have begun to affect the car at last. That the wet salt has been forced up into the body and has worked its way into the suspension. This means that the only thing we can do is to change the suspension units. This is a fairly complex operation and will take Leo Villa and his boys three days of solid work. After that I will be ready to run immediately. Believe me, gentlemen, no one regrets further delay at this point more than I do, but there is absolutely no alternative. Has anyone any questions?'

It was Wally Parr who spoke then, quietly, reasonably, reminding us all that for readers of newspapers, for anyone away from our tight, in-bred little group at Lake Eyre, what mattered was fact rather than belief or prejudice or emotion.

'What about *Bluebird*'s recorder, Donald? Surely it was running? What did it show of these vibrations you say you felt?'

'There you've got me, Wally,' replied Campbell. 'That's the very devil of it. We find we have perfect recordings for this morning's first two attempts, but for the one where the vibrations started the recorder had run out of film.'

'So you have no recording,' said Parr, putting away his pencil.

'So we have no recording.'

Once more it was the silence inside the tent that must have told Campbell what everyone was thinking. He and Mustard were staring directly at each other now—Campbell, his mouth pursed in anger, his eyes pale and very bright; Mustard, solemn, restrained.

'If anyone thinks that these vibrations were a figment of my imagination,' Campbell said, growling the words out like the challenge they were, 'they might be in a better position to judge such things if they had had some experience of the sort of speed at which I encountered them.'

And it was Brebner, tall, kindly, level-headed Brebner, the superintendent from the South Australian Police who was in charge of the troops manning the causeway, who had the last word before we went.

'If anyone can think of any funny stories to keep my boys amused during the next three days, perhaps they would leave them behind in writing.'

On this note of bitterness ended the meeting at the army camp.

9
Heir Apparent

It was very dark outside the tent. There were no stars and the night air was cold, colder than any night since we reached Lake Eyre.

'It's midwinter here now. It'll soon be June,' said the cameraman from the film unit as we walked back to the homestead. He was a large, red-faced man from Brisbane who had lived in the outback many years.

'Whatever he's up to he'll have to get a move on. There's rain on the way. I can smell rain. So can the flies. Have you seen how they've been coming indoors all day, and how the ants have been digging? It's always a sign. The rain's on its way.'

The wind had increased, shifted to the north-east, the rain quarter, and was humming in the big aerial over the homestead like raiding aircraft.

Leo Villa must have driven straight back from the meeting, for he was already in the kitchen drinking his last cup of tea before turning in. Behind him were the big white Frigidaire, the green painted cupboard around the rainwater tank, the crates of beer, cartons of green beans, tinned asparagus, Golden Shred, Johnnie Walker whisky. A large aluminium kettle was hissing somnolently on the black and silver cooking range. As he heaped his three teaspoons of sugar into his blue and white cup, the glare of the kitchen light showed up the neatly cropped silver hair above his ears. He yawned, tasted the tea, and looked very much at home.

'Worried?' he said. 'By this evening's caper? If you let things like that worry you, you'll never get very far in this game. I always tell Donald he takes too much notice of people.

'Now Donald's old man was different. Totally different. You should have seen how he handled the press. None of this having them around all the time, waiting to pick up any little thing that goes wrong. That wasn't Sir Malcolm. He'd have the press along when he was due to run—give them a drink—show them the car—answer any questions they'd got—very polite, very firm—then he'd look at his watch and say, "Well, gentlemen, if you will excuse us now I'm sure you'll understand we've work to do." And that'd be that. Very much the gentleman, Sir Malcolm. And I must say, the press used to know their place in those days.'

Leo Villa was a mechanic of the old school and this was his strength. For him the only real problems were mechanical ones. He had no doubts about Campbell, and if he said there were vibrations it was his job to find the cause.

'I said I'd see Donald through this record,' he said as he poured himself some more tea. 'After this I think I'll call it a day. Perhaps a bungalow in Devon. I'm sixty-five next birthday, and while I'm getting older the cars aren't getting any simpler.

'Take this present spot of nonsense. There's the whole bloody suspension to strip down. Terrible job. It's hard to explain but the suspension works on big pneumatic legs. There's one for each wheel. Wonderful idea, I'm not saying it isn't, but it's a bitch of a thing to work on and we've got to strip down the entire wheel assembly to reach them. That's what'll take the time.'

As he spoke the difference between him and Ken Norris became clearer than it had ever been—Norris the designer, the mathematician, with his graphs and his neat calculations, working out the problems of a world record as a complex application of aerodynamics: Villa preparing to solve the trouble with his hands, with three days' hard work and the experience of forty years behind him.

'As a piece of design the car is a masterpiece. But it's a devil to work on. If you'd just wanted a car to get the record you could have had something far simpler, but this thing's a laboratory on wheels. That gives you an awful lot that can go wrong, and if it does there's no latitude on anything. Everything in this car's calculated to a degree.'

He might have said more, but Campbell came in.

'Well, Unc. So there you are. I might have known.' He was smoking a large Havana cigar. The wind had blown his hair across his forehead. He smiled at Villa, put his hand on his shoulder and sat down beside him. Suddenly he looked very young, Villa very old.

'You know there's definitely rain on the way, Unc.' He smiled at Villa apologetically as if the rain, like everything else, was possibly his fault. 'You understand what that'll mean, don't you?'

Villa looked down at his cup, shrugged his shoulders almost imperceptibly, and in the silence that followed you could hear the ticking of the big Japanese kitchen clock, and the whisper of steam from the kettle on the range. When Campbell spoke at last he was no longer smiling. It was a very different Campbell from the man who had faced Andrew Mustard at the meeting.

'Unc, up at that meeting tonight. I was right wasn't I? I mean, there could have been no question of going on until we had found out what was really wrong?'

''Course not, Skipper. It'd have been bloody madness.'

'Well, the whole thing's come to that now. But you know I was right, don't you?'

The appeal for Villa's approval surprised me, but the old man seemed to find nothing odd in it, and simply looked at Campbell and said, 'Don't worry, Donald. We'll sort out whatever there is that needs looking at, and we'll start on that suspension first thing tomorrow morning. My alarm's set for five-thirty.'

'Well you must get your sleep then, Unc, and take it as easy as you can. Let the others do the heavy work. Nothing's worth crocking yourself up over.

'You know,' he went on when Villa had collected his towel and his toothbrush and his soap dish and gone off towards the bathroom, 'I wasn't joking about the car today. Believe me, old sport, I wasn't joking at all. When I hit those vibrations around three hundred it was like being on a vibro-massage machine going full pelt, and I've no idea how I kept control of the car. It was within a bee's whisker of going right off the track. I had it happen to me once and believe you me, once in a lifetime's quite enough for that sort of experience.'

It was as if he was talking now to convince himself, and the more he talked about the crash at Utah, the more doubts one had, the more substance he seemed to give to all the old rumours about his brain damage which had started spreading around the camp again. For where is the line dividing caution from cowardice? And suppose, just suppose, Campbell really was sick and the vibrations were the product of his sickness. How could you tell?

He must have known what I was thinking, for he smiled wearily and stubbed out the remains of his cigar and said, 'I know what everyone's saying, old boy. I'm not such a fool as some people seem to think, and I know that Mr Mustard would get in that cockpit tomorrow morning if I'd let him. I don't doubt his courage whatever some people say about mine. No, he'd put his foot down as I once put my foot down and—bingo.'

He spread his hands.

'I don't care overmuch what Mr Andrew Mustard does to himself at this stage of the game, but I do care about the car. It would grieve me to see nine years' work going down the drain.'

That evening everyone at Muloorina had his own views on Campbell's predicament, and the arguments went until the last lights flickered in the army camp and the beer was exhausted and the dogs stopped barking along the creek. Some sided with

Campbell. Others felt that the evening's meeting had been the equivalent of a declaration of war, and that the only question left now was how Campbell could be forced to allow his reserve driver to take over and get the record before the rains came.

Mustard himself was more reasonable..He is a man of some dignity. He was wearing his blue blazer and his flannel trousers and a white shirt. He had brushed his hair, and when he spoke he did so with the restraint and authority of an heir apparent during the final lunacy of an ailing king.

He received visitors in his caravan—a very snug, very orderly caravan with everything in its place—the telephone on the table, the bottle of Haig for guests, the neat pile of books and reports on Lake Eyre and on *Bluebird*, the files and notebooks and photograph albums, the map of the lake with the marks he had made from the aerial surveys. It was like a battle caravan, with the engaged neatness of the headquarters of a front-line commander.

'It's quite simple. I believe Campbell is scared,' he said, 'and when a man's as scared as he is, the slightest trouble gets magnified out of all proportion.'

'You've said all this to his face?' asked a commentator on assignment to the Australian Broadcasting Commission. He was a large, bald man who had arrived only that day and seemed slightly appalled at what he had wandered into.

'Of course I've told him. I told him the other evening and I gave him an ultimatum. I said that either he got on with the job within a week, or I would call a press conference to announce publicly that if he wasn't willing to go for the record, there were at least three people who were.'

'And you stick to that?' said the commentator slowly.

'Of course I do. Campbell is a man with a psychological block. He's no longer the same man who got the records in the boat. The closer he gets to the speed where he crashed at Utah, the more difficult it becomes for him to drive the car. I think the time has come for us to make sure that he does drive, or if he won't, that he gets out and lets someone else get on with it.'

'So you doubt these vibrations Campbell says he felt this afternoon?' asked the commentator.

'It's not a question of doubting them. Of course you get vibrations in a car going at that speed. Hell, man, you must expect some discomfort. All I know is that if you want a world record you must go through the hazards that are necessary to obtain it. You don't cry off at every minor setback.'

Watching him talk it was impossible to doubt his sincerity. There was no question of Andrew Mustard's passionate anxiety that *Bluebird* should get the record. There was no question of his own willingness to accept the risks this involved. And granted his assessment of Campbell's character and the state of his mind, there was no question that he was right.

But if he were wrong about Campbell?

'You'd be willing to drive the car as it is on that track, Andrew?' asked the commentator earnestly. 'You'd be willing to drive it yourself?'

'Tomorrow, sir. A lot of people have put a lot of money into this Bluebird Project and I think they should start getting their money's worth.'

The atmosphere at Muloorina changed now. There was a closeness in the air, a scrupulous politeness between the homestead and the army camp. For the first time people began to watch what they said, and all the extravagant, noisy arguments that had gone on in the beer tent at night were over. Suspicion started. It was a bad time.

Leo Villa was working all day at the lake on *Bluebird*'s suspension, and a second shift had been organised under Tom Scrimshire to carry on during the night. Whatever the outcome between Campbell and Mustard, *Bluebird* had to be ready now as soon as possible.

Then even this seemed pointless, for on the second night of the overhaul the rain finally arrived as the red-faced cameraman had said it would—heavy spots of rain from the harsh black clouds that had been streaming majestically all day from the north. It arrived at nine-fifteen, spasmodically at first, like isolated bullets being fired against the tin roof of the verandahh, then rattling with a sudden crescendo as the storm broke.

When it eased off a little I stood at the door of the homestead and as I smelled for the first time the unforgettable faint smell of wet saltbush blowing from the outback, the rain seemed a godsend. It would kill the record bid stone dead and I could feel nothing but relief that this bitter tournament would now be over.

I did not want to see Campbell destroy himself. I did not want to see Mustard do it either. And during the last few days the car seemed to have grown out of hand, to have turned into a monstrous presence on its dead lake, a sort of minotaur waiting for its sacrifices and bringing out the selfishness and the fear and the bitterness of everyone who believed in it.

But now the attempt would have to be abandoned and we could leave Lake Eyre and return to sanity.

The storm had subsided. It was fresh and cool, and I walked across from the homestead to the post office trailer to inquire if any aircraft was expected to make the journey down to Adelaide during the next few days.

Parr had just sent his copy through to his office in Sydney and was standing in the lighted doorway of the caravan. He wore his hat and watched the rain with an expression of bleak satisfaction.

'So we'll never know the answer, will we?' he said. 'We'll never know who was right, Donald Campbell or Andrew Mustard.'

'Does it matter?' I said.

'Yes, it does matter. I hate people giving me puzzles and then not letting me find out the answer.'

He stepped down from the caravan and strolled with me through the rain.

'What I find so satisfactory about literature is that you usually get an answer of sorts in the end. No writer would ever leave his characters in the state these people here are in.'

He stopped and looked across at the homestead. All the lights were on, and a car had just drawn up. The engine was still running and the headlights were on, throwing tapering shafts of yellow light through the rain. Then the doors of the homestead opened, car doors slammed, and the engine and the headlights were extinguished.

'That's Campbell now,' he said, 'just arrived back from the lake to tell everybody it's all over.'

We watched silently for a moment, both trying to imagine what was going on inside the homestead now that Campbell was there. Then the rain blew again and we started to walk towards Parr's hut.

'Do you really know the man at all?' he said. 'Do you know why he's in the record game, or the real truth about his father, or about the crash at Utah? Have you even made up your mind yet about those vibrations of his? I haven't. I can't even make up my mind whether he's a nut case or the one really sane man in the place.'

'Unless the car runs again now, you'll never know,' I said. 'If that's the price of knowing, I'd rather leave things as they are.'

'But what about Campbell?' said Parr, pushing his hat back on his head and dabbing at his forehead with his handkerchief. 'D'you think that's what he feels? Perhaps he'd like to know the answers too.'

By now it was hard to tell exactly what Campbell did feel. He looked defeated, grey faced, as he sat in the kitchen with Ken Norris. But appearances alone were no answer to the sort of questions Parr had asked. The rain was still on his face and his hair was straggled down his forehead.

Elliot Price came in.

'Well, you've got your rain, Elliot,' said Campbell flatly. 'You can have your extra sheep now. You've got the feed you needed for the next twelve months. You and the sheep have won.'

'Don't be so sure, Donald. I've a hunch it won't rain all that much on the lake this time. Often times it rains on the homestead hard but not on the lake. I'll bet you a pound, Don—a pound sterling if you like—that you don't have twenty points of rain on the lake during this twenty-four hours. And the bit of rain you have had will be just what you need to bind the surface of the salt together.

He stood a moment looking at Campbell. He had done his best and Campbell, appreciating this, smiled at him weakly and raised his hand.

'Okay, Elliot, you old rogue. A pound it is. But this is one bet you can't win.'

'You never know, Don,' replied Price as he closed the door behind him.

'Ken, old boy,' said Campbell when the old man had gone. 'I should never have come to this bloody place. Never.' He poured himself some whisky, a drink he almost never took. 'It was a total error of judgment from the very beginning. Nothing, not one blind, bloody thing has gone right since I first saw the place four years ago.'

He seemed to hunch forward over the table as he spoke, and the words came in a weary detached voice.

'Thank our lucky stars, I suppose, that we've still got the old boat. She's a bit ancient now, but she's still good for another crack at the water record. But there's absolutely no point in going on here with the car, is there? This rain's finished everything.'

Norris nodded but said nothing, and his silence was more impressive than if he had spoken. For after Campbell, he and his firm had more to lose from the decision to abandon the attempt than anyone. *Bluebird* might belong to Campbell, but the design had come from Norris and his brother and he had lived with it for many years. Now, through no fault of his, it would end up as one more design that never quite achieved its purpose.

Campbell must have realised this. 'Of course I'll hang on to the car, Ken,' he said. 'Perhaps we'll even be able to have a go with it on some other track one day. Next year for that matter. No reason why we shouldn't. But not here,' he said bitterly, 'never again here.'

But as it turned out, Elliot Price was to win his bet. By some freak of the weather the storm veered away from the lake and only three points of rain, three hundredths of an inch, actually fell on the track—enough to delay things yet again, to make the surface just that much more treacherous, but not enough to finish everything once and for all. And when Leo Villa had finished the overhaul at the end of the third day, he said he could find nothing that really accounted for the vibrations.

'So you still don't know what caused them?' said Parr the following evening when he stopped Norris on the verandah after dinner.

'No, we're not sure, although I've an idea of my own what it is.'

'And what's that?'

'I'd rather keep it to myself until after tomorrow morning's run. I could easily be wrong. At any rate, Leo seems to have ruled out anything being wrong with the car.'

'And you've no doubt at all that Campbell really did feel these vibrations of his.'

'No doubt at all.'

'But aren't you asking him, then, to do something extremely dangerous tomorrow morning if he drives into the vibration belt again?'

'Of course. This whole business is extremely dangerous. Not everybody seems to appreciate it though.'

'And does he really understand the risk he's taking?'

'He understands all right. But if he's going to get the record we've got to find out what caused the trouble first, and if you've any ideas how we can do that without running *Bluebird* at three hundred tomorrow morning, I'd be very glad to hear them.'

10

The Uncertain Victory

So it was that on the morning of Wednesday 27 May, Campbell—grey-faced, hunch-shouldered, with two cups of coffee and a helping of cornflakes in his stomach—drove down to Lake Eyre at six-fifteen for his next speed trials. Much was at stake. The truth about the vibrations, for one thing; the outcome of his battle with Andrew Mustard, for another; the whole question of his mental condition for yet another.

The night before he had promised publicly (a thing he always disliked doing) that he intended to achieve 'several runs around the three hundred mile an hour mark to give Ken Norris and the engineers the readings they need before we can proceed to higher speeds'.

This time the film cassettes on *Bluebird*'s recorder had been checked and re-checked. The timekeepers would be there. There would be no misunderstandings.

All this showed on Campbell's face as he waited by the hangar while the mechanics made their last adjustments to *Bluebird* on that grey morning. They took no longer than usual, but now each stage in the final preparations seemed one more attempt to prolong his ordeal.

The controls were checked—the air pressure for his pneumatic brakes—the compressed air he breathed in the cockpit for the three or four minutes of the run—the valve controlling the percentage of power from the turbine.

'There's a wind of three knots, south-east, Don,' shouted Carl Noble. 'Shouldn't worry you.'

'We've given you sixty per cent power on the turbine,' said Norris. 'That'll be more than enough. Take her up steadily to three hundred, then see what happens. If you get the vibrations hold her as long as you can before bringing her down. If not, take her on up.'

Campbell nodded. The check-through was nearly over, and Tonia was waiting near the car with the blue holdall, when Andrew Mustard arrived from inspecting the track in his red racing car. He wore a clean pair of white overalls with his name on the back.

'Morning, Andy, old boy. Everything all right?' said Campbell.

Mustard took off his sunglasses and smiled. 'Good morning Donald. At the moment the track is perfect. We've been going over the surface once more this morning with the drags, and you have twelve and three-quarter miles. I believe it's as smooth now as you'll ever get it. Whatever was causing those vibrations of yours, I don't think you'll find it's the track.'

'Let's hope not, Andy. Let's hope not.'

As usual before a run, Campbell seemed a solitary, strangely lonely figure. Perhaps it was the imminent possibility of death which isolated him from the rest of us. The risk he was about to take made conversation difficult, as I realised when I found myself standing next to him.

'You know,' he said suddenly, 'I'd give almost anything to be a thousand miles away from here at the moment.' He looked down at the salt and neither of us spoke. The mechanics had nearly finished now and Tonia was waiting by the cockpit.

'It's not so much the business of being afraid,' he said, 'although fear's one thing you never get used to. You can't train yourself to endure fear as you might to endure hunger. Fear's always bad, every time. But it's not that that worries me, old scout, it's just the strain of this whole bloody business. I'm not sure I can take it much longer or that I even want to take it much longer.'

'Ready now, Skipper?' shouted Leo Villa from the front of the car.

'Coming, Unc. Coming,' said Campbell quietly, but as we started walking towards the car he went on, 'You see, if you're going to take a record in a machine like this you really have to want it. You have to want it with your whole being just as you have to want a woman if you're going to make her properly. With this record, I've reached the point where I'm not sure that I want to make it any more.'

'Compressor on. Ready when you are,' shouted Carl Noble.

'She's all yours, Skipper,' said Villa, unfastening the safety cable which held open the cockpit canopy.

'The trouble is,' said Campbell as he untied the laces of his suede desert boots, 'there's only a certain amount the old nervous system can stand and I reckon I've just about got there.'

All record bids are the same and yet all are different. There is the same noise, the same car, the same smell of burning fuel and hot metal as the booster comes on and the turbine whirrs and the engine thunders to life—the same last-minute cockpit checks and scurrying away of mechanics like anxious hospital orderlies in their surgical white overalls.

And the differences? The differences are that each run marks a different stage in the record breaker's ordeal and that of the few men sharing it with him.

During the first run that morning I watched Norris and Villa. They were together in the car in which we followed *Bluebird* along the track. The Valiant was doing over ninety, and as they squinted through the windscreen along the glaring white track ahead, it must have been very like the other ninety-mile-an-hour dash they made together four years before at Utah as *Bluebird* disappeared over the horizon. I remembered the words from Norris's report when that dash was over.

'We were doing a good ninety mph. The past kept imposing itself with endless accusations. You should have done this and that and that.'

But whatever self-accusations Norris had now, he was keeping to himself. So was Leo Villa. They sat quite still, their faces masks, and it was not until we had reached the far end of the track and the Valiant had skidded to a halt that their anxiety showed for just a moment as they leapt from the car and rushed across to Campbell.

He looked battered and even worse than before the run.

'Well, the vibrations are still there,' he said. 'Hit me just past three-ten.'

'Bad as ever?' asked Villa.

'Not quite, but I still thought I was going to get my eyes shaken out of my head.'

Instead of getting out of the car as he usually did. Campbell sat where he was, and gradually a crowd collected as the rest of the cars arrived. Once again his weird ability to impose his mood on the people round him began to show itself. Because he was quiet, everyone else was too. Voices were lowered.

'Was it bad, darling?' Tonia asked, leaning over the edge of the car.

He nodded.

'You'd think it was a funeral,' said one of the cameramen.

'That's just what it is,' murmured Wally Parr beneath his breath. 'But I'm interested in Ken Norris. I've an idea that if anyone knows the answer to all this, he does.'

While Parr was speaking, Norris had left the side of the cockpit and walked slowly towards the back of the car. There was no one else there, and we watched him as he bent down by one of the rear wheels and carefully ran his finger round the inside of the rim. Then he walked to the other side of the car and did the same.

Whatever he had found, he seemed to be keeping to himself. We watched him open his brown folder, scribble some figures in pencil, scratch his head and then walk away.

'I'd like to know just what he's up to,' said Parr. 'Let's go and look at those wheels for ourselves.'

Bluebird's wheels are enormous. The tyres are completely smooth, made up of layer upon layer of rayon and wafer-thin rubber, and the rim of the wheel is a couple of inches deep. Parr bent down and ran his thumb along the bottom of the rim as we had seen Norris doing.

'Very interesting,' he said. 'Just look at that.' When he held out his thumb I saw that it was covered in something thick and white like toothpaste.

'You'd hardly believe it, would you,' he said.

'What is it?'

'Salt, I suppose. With the wet on the surface of the track it must be getting thrown up by the speed of the wheels and then packing against the rims. It's quite thick.'

We walked towards the front of the car where the inquest on the run was still in progress. Andrew Mustard was there now and most of the engineers. Leo Villa was explaining why the source of the vibrations could not lie in the suspension.

'Are you sure that the recorder was operating that time?' asked Mustard. But nobody answered, and nobody seemed to know whether Campbell would make another run now or not.

'Andrew,' said Norris suddenly. 'I think we should change the wheels.'

Mustard was the official Dunlop representative. Under the arrangement Campbell had with the company, Mustard was responsible to him, but the wheels and tyres which Dunlops had developed specially for the car remained their property.

'Certainly, Ken, if you think it can help, although all the wheels have been checked for balance and accuracy countless times, as you know.'

'I know. But I'd like to see what happens if we change them all the same.'

So the wheels were changed. *Bluebird* could raise itself on four pneumatic rams which came sliding from beneath its belly at the touch of a button. These rams were one of Campbell's own ideas which Norris had skilfully incorporated in the design, and on the actual record bid, as a matter of course, the wheels would be switched between the first and second runs.

The four panels at the side of the car where lifted off, exposing the great convex silver discs of the wheels. The rams came down, and silently, effortlessly, *Bluebird* raised herself a further two inches off the ground. The fresh wheels were pushed forward on small, yellow tubular steel trolleys, and when the hub bolts had been undone and the old wheels removed, the new ones were lifted carefully into place and bolted home. The whole operation took something less than ten minutes. Then *Bluebird* gently lowered itself again like a large fish in the act of mating, and the rams slid back into its body.

'Now, Andrew,' said Norris, 'would you make sure that the rims have been wiped absolutely clear of all trace of salt?'

'But they are clean. They're fresh wheels.'

'Good,' said Norris, and the wheel panels were fixed back into position.

Campbell started putting on his helmet once more, and Leo Villa stood by the cockpit talking earnestly.

'Looks as if we are having another run after all,' said Parr. 'This is going to be important. Let's take the car and get right up the track so we see what happens when he gets to the other end.'

So we took one of the trucks and drove off along the service road that ran along the length of the main track, passing the big red marker at the start of the measured mile and the caravan with the slender aluminium aerial where the timekeepers lived. We waited ten minutes until *Bluebird* had flashed by with the unearthly sound of its acceleration, half whine, half roar. It appeared faster than we had seen it before.

'Let's find out what's happened,' said Parr. He started the engine and we raced off in pursuit. But on the way the grey Valiant passed us with Norris and Villa aboard, and we reached the *Bluebird* in time to see Campbell handing the crash helmet to Norris and levering himself out of the cockpit. He was smiling faintly to himself but making no attempt to talk.

'Well, Skipper,' said Villa anxiously, 'how was that one?'

'Not so bad, Unc,' said Campbell softly. 'Not so bad.'

'What sort of speed?'

'Something just over three hundred.'

'And the vibrations?' asked Norris. 'Did you feel them again?'

'No, Ken. Not a sign. She behaved beautifully.'

Norris's caravan at Muloorina had been parked at the back of the homestead next door to the bungalow where one of Elliot's daughters lived with her family. And it was in this caravan that he spent almost the rest of that day working on the film that had come out of *Bluebird*'s recorder. Ken Reaks and Carl Noble helped him develop it and festoon it across the caravan to dry. When I called on them just after five, Ken Reaks was setting up the small film projector used for examining the film, a frame at a time.

'So he *was* right about the vibrations,' I said.

'Sure. He was right all along, and he was even right at the very beginning when he diagnosed wheel unbalance. The film shows it quite clearly. As soon as old Reaks has got his projector working I'll let you see for yourself. The vibrations were very bad. He was lucky to get away with it.'

'But why did they vanish on the final set this morning? Was there something wrong with the first set of wheels?'

'No, the wheels themselves were perfectly all right. All that was happening was that over several runs the wet salt had been drying unevenly inside the rims and making them just a fraction out of balance. I suspected wheel trouble too when Don complained of the vibrations, but Andrew was so insistent that they were all perfectly balanced. I should have thought of the salt drying unevenly before. It was only this morning that I twigged it.'

'What I still don't understand, Ken, is how a few spoonfuls of salt can make all that difference,' said Reaks. Reaks is a small, jolly man with bright blue eyes and a very large moustache. He has been supervising Campbell's instrumentation since the days of his record bids with the boat on Coniston Water.

'Well, at the speed those wheels travel, a couple of ounces out of balance would make all the difference,' replied Norris. 'If you've got the projector working now I'll show you what two ounces of salt can do.'

The projector was plugged in, and threw a bright yellow rectangle a yard across on the far wall of the caravan.

'Here,' said Norris, feeding the first strip of film through the machine. 'At this point *Bluebird*'s travelling at around a hundred and twenty. You see the lines from all four suspensions are pretty straight. The only fluctuation comes from one or two bumps along the track. Nothing to worry about at that speed. The top black line is the steering movement. You see it's absolutely straight.'

He pushed his hair back, and leaned over to feed the film on.

'Here he is just past the second mile mark, doing about two hundred and forty.' He traced the bottom suspension line across the screen with his finger. 'He was taking her up very steadily, and you can see there's still nothing much to worry about. Ideally, of course, you'd like all the lines to be straight, but these variations are all right. But here,' he said as he wound more film on, 'here's where the real trouble begins. At about two-ninety, three and a half miles down the track.'

From the picture on the wall it looked as if the recorder had suddenly developed St Vitus's dance, for each of the black lines for the suspension had become jagged and even the steering line fluctuated sharply.

'It must have been a terrible job to keep her on the track at all,' he said, pointing to the top line. 'You can see what the vibrations were doing to the steering.'

'But it'll be all right now,' said Reaks.'

'Sure,' said Norris, 'it'll be all right now.'

And it was all right—more than all right. On the surface at any rate. The following morning Campbell drove again and went his fastest yet, and for the first time since he had been at Lake Eyre the record seemed within reach.

It was a great moment when the run was over. He sat on the back of the cockpit, grinning as he took off his crash helmet, and winked at Ken Norris.

'She's not an easy car to drive, but she goes. I'll say that for you, Ken. This car of yours is a goer.'

Just as we had shared in all the previous failures, so now success was here for everyone. Norris beamed, giving Campbell his shy, hair-encumbered smile.

'Well, Don. You can't have everything. Any vibrations that time?'

'No. Nothing like we had before.'

'What speed d'you think, Skipper?' asked Villa proudly.

'Off the record, Unc, I'd say three forty-five, but I may be right up the wall.'

He changed from the blue gym shoes to the suede desert boots, slid down on to the salt, and kissed Tonia on both cheeks. They looked young and successful. And when the official speed from the timekeepers came over the radio—352 miles an hour through the measured mile—Campbell kissed his wife again.

As they were walking away I heard Parr's voice from the radio on the Morris 1100 repeating the news back to Muloorina for transmission over to the Australian Associated Press office in Adelaide.

The loudspeakers made his voice sound high pitched and not quite human. '... three five two miles an hour officially timed. The nearest to Campbell's highest speed on land when he crashed four years ago at Utah at three six zero.'

There was a very short meeting that night and the atmosphere was discreet. There was no sign of excitement, even when Campbell announced that after his run that day he had telephoned Mr Don Thomson, secretary of the Club of Australian Motor Sports, requesting that official stewards be sent to Lake

Eyre as soon as possible.

There were no congratulations, no spontaneous admissions of error. Campbell looked tired and clearly had no great wish to stay talking for long.

'So you could get the record on Saturday, Don,' said a voice.

Campbell smiled. 'Let us not be premature, gentlemen.'

11

Omens

It was as Campbell left the meeting that Norris stopped him. 'Don, I'm worried. Something rather dreadful's happened. Just had a telephone call from Marjorie. The baby's coming earlier than we expected. I'm desperately worried. If anything happened and I wasn't there, I'd never forgive myself.'

'But I thought it was the second week in June the baby was due.'

'So did we. Marjorie wouldn't say much on the phone but I'm afraid something might have gone wrong.'

'Well, there's no question about it then. You must get back to England right away.'

'I'm sorry about it, Don. It's the worst possible moment for this to happen, but I'm worried stiff about them at home.'

'Of course I understand. Your family's got to come first. I'll fly you down to Adelaide first thing tomorrow morning, it'll do me good to get away from here for a day. But what about analysing the recordings from the last runs? Can you finish that before you go?'

'I'll stay up tonight and finish them. The car seems to be behaving perfectly now, and I can't see that any further adjustments will be needed, but if anything does crop up after I've left, Carl Noble can work out the mathematics as well as I can.'

'No one knows the car as you do, Ken. We shall miss you. Believe me, we'll miss you.'

Campbell put his hand on his shoulder and the two of them walked to the blue Humber in which Campbell had driven to the meeting.

'One thing we might do, Ken,' he said. 'When we get back to the homestead, why not telephone through to your doctor. With a baby on the way a lot of things can get exaggerated over twelve thousand miles, and he might be able to set your mind at rest a little.'

The operator at Adelaide had reported an hour's delay on all calls to London, and Norris, looking really worried for the first time since he reached Lake Eyre, had gone back to the caravan to work on his analysis until the telephone rang. Campbell waited too. He settled himself into the blue deckchair on the verandah and gloomily lit a large cigar.

'I don't like this,' he said. 'I don't like any of it. I'm fetching the stewards up now because I've got to, but we're not really ready for the record yet, not by a long chalk. I'm not even going to get those fifteen runs I wanted.'

He puffed hard at the cigar. Large, white-bellied moths were clinging to the mosquito wire behind his head.

'I've got to make an attempt within the next few days. I can't afford the expense of the thing dragging on much longer, and in a week most of the engineers will have to get back to their firms in England. The weather's breaking. I don't know why. According to statistics, December should be the wettest month and the wind doesn't usually come until July. Now there's this business with Ken,' he said. It really is as though something's against me.'

He put his left hand behind his neck and pushed his head back as far as it would go.

'Hell, it's stiff,' he said. He went on smoking, and the moths clambered awkwardly up towards the light. Occasionally one would loose its grip and slither down the wire.

'There was only one occasion when I saw my father afraid. I've never forgotten it. That was at Utah too—funny the way our paths keep crossing—Utah in 1935. He was there with his new car, two and a half thousand horse-power. She was to be his last *Bluebird* car, and he'd set his heart on being the first man to travel at over three hundred on land. He took me with him to Salt Lake City. I was at Uppingham still. I was pretty sick of school, and it was the greatest treat of my life, for I really worshipped the old man, you know.

'I was there when he made his first run through the measured mile on the record bid, and something went wrong. When Leo and I reached *Bluebird* after the run, one of the front tyres was burning and he was standing by the car looking deathly pale.'

Campbell had told me the same story some time before, but he must have forgotten, for the whole experience was a key passage in his career, and as he went on I was fascinated to see how he was repeating himself word for word.

'I said, "What happened, Dad?"

'"Nearside front tyre burst when I had her going at three hundred and four,' he replied. But that wasn't all. Exhaust fumes had been coming into the cockpit and he'd nearly passed out. He looked very grim. "Will the run back be all right, Dad?" I asked. "Have to be, boy. Have to be." That was all he said. When the tyre was changed he climbed back into the cockpit and got the record. That's the sort of man he was.'

Campbell paused and looked up. 'You know, I've never forgotten the way he looked at me as he said those words. But now I'm in the game myself I know what it was. He thought he'd had it.'

The telephone rang, and Norris came from the caravan to take the call in the Prices' sitting room. Campbell, silent now, stayed on in the deckchair, finishing the cigar.

At last the door opened and Norris came out. He looked at Campbell and smiled a little.

'Well, Ken,' said Campbell, 'what's the verdict?'

'The specialist says now that it definitely won't be until the weekend. Marjorie's comfortable and I'm to phone again tomorrow morning. It looks as though I've a day or two more here at any rate.'

'Thanks, Ken. Perhaps there is a chance after all.'

'Sit perfectly still, hands by your sides, and breathe in and out deeply as fast as you can like this.'

The small man in the combat uniform of an RAAF flight lieutenant was breathing with quite startling power and rapidity, and Campbell, sitting beside him on a brown kitchen chair, began doing the same.

It was the next evening and we were at the homestead. The stewards were due by charter plane from Melbourne some time the following morning. Ken Norris had been told by his doctor that the immediate anxiety for his wife was over. And since the news of the stewards' arrival had leaked out, a whole crop of visitors was expected for the weekend. Campbell had spent the day visiting the lake, and now after dinner he had asked the newly arrived medical officer, Dr Denis Burke, over for a drink.

Burke, an Adelaide GP, was on the air force reserve and had been sent to Lake Eyre as medical officer. As we discovered that evening, he had pronounced views of his own on the subject of aviation medicine. These views, as Campbell learned later, did not always coincide with official air force policy.

He was a powerful talker, with earnest brown eyes and a strong Irish jaw, and he and Campbell found a subject of immediate mutual interest in the causes of the crash at Utah. Campbell described to him the symptoms of his loss of control before the crash.

'Sounds like a perfectly straightforward case of hyperventilation,' said Burke. 'The carbon dioxide level in the blood gets lowered dangerously through overbreathing. In your case the oxygen you inhaled would have been the primary factor. We often get cases of this with pilots under stress. Used to be a serious cause of unexplained accidents until we learned what was happening. Causes the pilot to lose all sense of judgment and most of his skill. Acute cases of hyperventilation seem to have no sense of danger or personal involvement with what they're doing.'

Burke spoke with the assured enthusiasm doctors sometimes show when embarked upon their favourite theories, but Campbell had already discussed hyperventilation with experts in England and America.

'Of course, in my case, it was the fact of inhaling pure oxygen at sea level that caused the crash,' he said.

'Probably,' replied Burke, 'but that needn't necessarily have been the only factor. These things vary from individual to individual, according to the personal blood chemistry. All the symptoms you had may have been due simply to overbreathing.'

'You mean it could happen again,' said Campbell, 'even though I'm no longer using oxygen?'

'Cases have been known,' replied Burke, 'of subjects overbreathing under stress and showing very similar symptoms to those you just described.'

'For crying out loud,' said Campbell.

'I've known several cases of combat pilots,' added Burke, 'and the American space project people have had to face the same phenomenon—overbreathing in time of high nervous tension, resulting in acute lowering of the carbon dioxide level in the blood. 'It's very simple to correct. Carbon dioxide's the answer. Just a whiff. Completely restores the CO_2 level in the blood. You'd be surprised how swiftly the symptoms of hyperventilation vanish. Remarkable stuff, CO_2. I've used it to banish symptoms of the common cold, and I've used it with effect in cases of rheumatism.'

Dr Burke sat back. His face had turned rather pink, and he regarded Campbell with every sign of satisfaction. 'I think,' he added, 'that we should know what effect overbreathing has on you.'

So the experiment began.

Campbell kept up the breathing for about a minute. His face was tense and grew rapidly paler; his knuckles showed white as he gripped the arms of the chair. His breathing was like that of a woman in advanced childbirth.

'Very well, Donald. How do you feel?' asked Dr Burke in a reassuring medical voice. 'Any change yet?'

'Slight tingling in the hands and feet.'

'Very good. Carry on please, Donald.'

'Now, Donald,' he said a few seconds later. 'Maintain your breathing rate, but would you mind getting up and walking round the room. Take your time.'

With some uncertainty, Campbell got to his feet and still breathing as heavily as ever, navigated his way past the green sofa, the large yellow dumpty, the standard lamp, the piano and the television set. His movements were stiff but determined, his face preoccupied. He failed to notice the small coffee table, but Dr Burke was there to take his arm and guide him back to his chair.

'Very good, Donald, *very* good. And now I would like you to read me something from this newspaper.' He gave him the front page of a recent copy of the *Adelaide Advertiser* and Campbell started off on the lead story. In place of the customary crisp, faintly arrogant diction the words were now laboured and slurred.

'Excellent. Now would you please write your name and address on this sheet of paper.'

As Campbell picked up the biro and began to write, he was clearly having to make an enormous effort. It was as if his arm was stiff and his mind drugged. And instead of the usually flamboyant signature, his writing wavered across the page like a very old man's, but he was determined to finish.

'Very well, Donald. Now stop, and breathe normally. Slowly. Slowly. That's better.'

Recovery was swift. Within five minutes Campbell was back to normal and anxiously discussing his symptoms.

'I wouldn't say extreme,' said Dr Burke, 'but a pronounced reaction. You remember the way you went on stubbornly trying to finish the writing? That's another symptom of hyperventilation we found in pilots. They would just go on with some pointless activity, not seeming to realise it was no use at all.'

'What would you suggest in my case then, doctor?' asked Campbell.

'Well, in the first place, don't worry about it. Worry's the very worst thing you can do. But practise shallow breathing. When you're in the cockpit avoid those deep breaths you take under stress. And I think I'd better see if I can't get you some compressed CO_2. You can inhale it just before a run, and it will stop any chance of hyperventilation. Best to be on the safe side.'

But Tonia was worried about the idea of giving him CO_2. 'We're getting very near the edge now,' she said. 'If any man can do it he will, but there's an awful lot against him. This is his battle and he's the only one who can fight it.'

Next day, after breakfast, Elliot Price called on Campbell.

'Let me take you round some of my land, Don. You can bring your guns with you and do a bit of shooting. Take your mind off things.'

Campbell had begun playing patience again. As a rule he dislikes being disturbed in a game, but Price's suggestion appealed to him.

'Excellent idea, Elliot, old sport. Wait while I get a couple of guns and some ammunition.' He went off in the direction of the bedroom, and when he appeared on the verandah a few minutes later in his blue Ampol battle-dress jacket with a rifle over each shoulder he looked cheerful for the first time for days. His hair stuck up and his eyes sparkled. He had a truant look about him.

'Come on, Elliot, quick. Let's get out of here.'

We borrowed the big grey Valiant, shabby now with dust and the salt from the lake. Campbell took great care as he piled the rifles with their gleaming blue barrels into the boot along with the special slings and telescopes and cleaning rods and binoculars and the heavy neat boxes of ammunition. He likes equipment, the more expensive the better. He likes radios and knives and good cameras and machine tools. He has a beautifully kept collection of firearms at his house in Surrey. The mere act of handling the guns as he placed them in the boot seemed to give him pleasure.

We drove eastwards from the homestead. The worn red carpet of the airstrip lay to our right. For a moment we could see the homestead buildings behind us. They looked delicate and impracticable, like toy sheds and farms and wind-pumps placed in a wilderness for some game and then forgotten. Then the car pitched forward. The homestead vanished behind a ridge and we were alone in the most ravaged landscape in the world. It was a flat grey land where every particle of life had been scorched away leaving this inert cinder country where the only noise was the wind scouring the low, hide-coloured rocks and carrying the dust for miles in long clouds going from nowhere to nowhere.

From the front seat of the Valiant, Elliot Price regarded it with satisfaction.

'Some of my best land, this, Donald,' he said, pulling back his shoulders and scratching his chest. 'Know how much the bastards on the Land Board charges now? Three and nine, Donald. Three and bloody ninepence a square mile.'

Campbell said nothing, and as we jolted on Price began talking about the one real enthusiasm of his life—his land—pointing out the all but invisible grey scrub, the endlessly surviving small plants which could keep sheep alive even here—the copper burr, the black-blue bush, the marsh saltbush—'good tucker for the sheep, Don, though Christ knows how they eat it'.

But even here Campbell was unable to forget Lake Eyre. There was no escape, not for him at any rate, and when Price stopped talking to concentrate on the way ahead, he suddenly began telling me what a strain the last few days had been.

'It's not nerves,' he said quietly, 'and it's not fear either. I know everyone gets nerves, but this is something different. It's only come on this week. It's a constant tension and I'm terrified it's going to impair my judgment. It makes me want to seize up completely. I was exhausted after that last run at three-fifty the other day, completely exhausted. I slept five hours straight off, and

I've never done that before.'

'Look, Donald,' said Price, interrupting to point out a row of white wooden skeletons of trees along the horizon. 'Coolibah trees. That's how they was along the Cooper the time they'd had no rain for thirty-six years. Dead as buggery they looked. Then the rains come and the leaves start all over again.'

We passed a big stained concrete water-tank holding water for the sheep, pumped through iron piping from a bore hole ten miles away, and he told us how the man who had supervised the work on the pipeline had been living at this very spot in a caravan with his young wife eighteen months earlier.

'Beautiful girl she was. Beautiful girl. And seven months gone when she had this miscarriage. Happened at night, it did, right here. And she bled to death in his arms. Then two days later the poor bugger's in Marree arranging her funeral and a kerosene fridge he's left on in the caravan catches light and burns the whole thing to a cinder. Look, Don, over there.'

He stopped the car and pointed a hundred yards or so beyond the tank to where the scrub was blackened by an ancient blaze and there were still strips of twisted iron.

'Poor devil was in a terrible state, didn't eat a thing or stop crying for a fortnight. In two days flat he'd lost his wife, his caravan and everything he had. Went off without a penny except what we could give him.'

The story seemed to impress Campbell, and he insisted on leaving the car to inspect the place where the death and the blaze occurred. 'You see the sort of country this is,' he said as he turned the rusting angle-iron over with his foot. 'No mercy in it. A cruel land. A cruel terrible land. Was there nothing he could do for the girl, Elliot, nothing at all?'

'No, Don. She just bled and that was an end to her.'

We chose a spot nearby for our target practice, sticking tin cans on the ground at two and three hundred yards and using the bonnet of the car to rest the rifles. Campbell shot better than anyone but he did not speak at all.

12

'A hair's breadth thing'

The first Saturday in June around three-thirty in the afternoon a
thin bony old man with white hair and bright earnest eyes was
standing on the verandah of the homestead talking to Campbell.
His shirt was stained. His grey trousers had been intended for a
stomach many sizes larger than his. He had driven two hundred
and fifty miles across country from Oodnadatta, the legendary cattle
town to the north, and his antique red Dodge truck was standing,
still quivering from the strain of the journey, in front of the house.

'Mr Campbell?'

'Yes, sir. What can I do for you, sir?'

'Mr Campbell. Me'n my boy've just drove to see you get the
record. Reck'n we'll see anything if we stays around?'

'Well, sir, I can't promise anything. I would say it could take
anything up to another week. You can't rush these things you
know.'

'But me'n the boy thought we'd be seeing something this
weekend.'

'Well, wait around, sir, and we'll see what we can do. It all
depends on the weather and the state of the lake. Wait around, sir.
Wait around.'

And everyone else at Muloorina waited around, convinced that if they could last out for one more weekend they would see some action. Campbell would not say what his plans were or what he was going to do. He seemed to have an almost superstitious horror now of committing himself to anything, promising anything, before he had actually done it. But however unprepared he might be for an all-out record bid, and whatever the state of the salt or the track, it had become tacitly accepted that he would have to try now or never. The circus had to begin, and from the previous evening a new audience had been arriving at Muloorina to see it.

There was something uncanny about the way new faces suddenly appeared, making this closed society we had endured so long suddenly public. That Saturday we had woken to see tents pitched between the wattle bushes and the sand dunes around the homestead. Caravans had arrived. Four post office workers at a Friday night ball in Adelaide had taken a bet at midnight and driven non-stop, arriving dazed, dirty and fifty pounds to the good, just after nine on Saturday morning. The landing-strip had graduated overnight to a minor airport. By Saturday lunchtime there were a dozen planes lining its western perimeter—two Aero Commanders, a maroon Cessna from South Australian Air Taxis, a yellow Aztec, a blue and white Beechcraft, a Sky-waggon from Nicholas Air Charter.

Each fresh plane load gave Campbell another reason for putting his foot down that weekend. One of the planes had come all the way from Sydney with MacLeonard, the general manager of the Ampol oil company. By training MacLeonard was an accountant, a short quiet man with a way of thrusting his hands into the pockets of his neat gaberdine golf jacket and looking at you and making it clear from his very silence that he was in the habit of getting value for his money. Mason, his deputy general manager, had come on the same plane—tall, good-looking Mason, an ex-naval commander and still the right side of forty-five, very English and very anxious in the nicest possible way that Campbell should get the record now before too long. For Mason had had a lot to do with

Ampol's decision to back Campbell and the company had much at stake.

Then there were the other plane visitors. There was a very tall, silent millionaire from Melbourne with a beautiful wife who wore ski pants and a black leather coat and talked a lot. There was Florence, who had got back from Jakarta with her divorce and had flown up with champagne so that we could all celebrate her freedom and Campbell's record in one splendid party. And there were Grand Prix drivers like Lex Davison and Bib Stilwell who had come out of interest in this car of Campbell's which would try for the record at four times the speed at which they had made their own reputations in their Lotuses and Ferraris.

Before this weekend Campbell had been operating in private. All the rows and all the anxieties had been in a sense private rows and private anxieties. Now he was in public, officially billed for a performance he was unofficially insisting was not ready to start, and that Saturday his visitors and his well-wishers were like an audience turning up for a play while the rehearsals are still going on, while the playwright is arguing about the lines, and the principal actor is having doubts about whether he can go through with it.

'It shouldn't have happened like this,' he said. 'The old man wouldn't have let it happen like this. But then Father was always independent, and he was far too wise to take on anything quite like Lake Eyre. It was all so much simpler in his day and age, old boy, and the old man was always in a much stronger position than I am to say exactly when he was going to do something.'

It was the contrast between the pressures which were on him now and the independence his father enjoyed in his record breaking which made his situation so galling. He felt trapped now as he had not felt trapped before. All along he had been trying to assert one thing—his right to run for the record when he was ready to run and not a moment before. All along he had been trying not to gamble any more than he had to. But now he was caught.

The story Elliot had told us the day before about the man with the caravan near the bore tank seemed to be on his mind too.

'Terrible story, but that's what can happen to you in a place like this. All in the space of a few hours. You lose everything, everything you possess. Your life is ruined. It's that sort of country. Either you beat it as Elliot has done, or it beats you.'

But whatever doubts Campbell was having now about himself and the state of his nerves, he was keeping to himself, and for a man as worried as he was his performance that afternoon, welcoming his visitors, laughing at their jokes, evading the one question they all wanted to ask him, was remarkable.

But that same afternoon he was having other discussions too. He spent a long time with Ken Norris talking about the car and what was to be done. For Norris the situation was hardly less of a nightmare than it was for Campbell. *Bluebird* was his design. He was the only one who really understood it. Its behaviour at high speeds was still untested, and Norris was in the position of a scientist working with insufficient data and a man's life at stake.

For the past two or three days he had been involved in his calculations, plotting the suspension readings from *Bluebird*'s recorder on to graph paper and attempting to find out from the way the car had behaved at three hundred miles an hour how she was likely to react at four hundred plus. He was very neat with these sums. Each of *Bluebird*'s runs had its separate sheet in his file, and each was analysed and compared with the readings of what had gone before. But none of this was really enough in the freak conditions the car was having to encounter. The closer *Bluebird* got towards four hundred, the further it would get from the predictable area covered by the graphs and the equations.

It was a strange conversation the two of them had, strange because of the offhand, almost casual way the two men talked as they sat in the small office at the back of the homestead, with its one small shuttered window and its cream-painted deal table one of Elliot's daughters used when she did the accounts for the sheep station. There was Norris in his maroon aertex shirt and his baggy brown trousers, a diffident, very quiet man whose moustache, like the sort of moustaches students grow, succeeded only in making him look even younger than he was; and Campbell as eager, as amiable as ever, with his double-breasted blue blazer specially put on to meet his visitors that afternoon.

No one seeing them here for the first time would have believed that they had any connection with what they were actually doing. It was as difficult to imagine Norris designing anything as complex, as beautiful, as deadly as the car *Bluebird*, as to think of the man opposite him getting ready to kill himself in it.

'How much power may I use, Ken?'

'Depends on the state of the lake in the morning. If it's dry enough and we can get sufficient adhesion for the wheels, I should try it up to ninety-five per cent. At that I reckon you should have all the acceleration you want to get up to four twenty by the sixth mile.'

'Provided the salt takes it.'

'Provided the salt takes it. That's what worries me. The adhesion can change a couple of points in half an hour, and I don't have to tell you what happens if you lose adhesion when accelerating on ninety-five per cent power.'

'No, old sport, you don't have to tell me at all.' Campbell lit himself a cigarette, inhaled deeply, and looked hard at Norris. The memory of Utah was still dogging them. There was no need to repeat what happened when a car lost adhesion approaching four hundred.

'So you'll leave it to the morning before you make a final decision on the power?' said Campbell at last.

'I think that's the only way,' said Norris, and went on to say that as far as he could see the other uncertainties about the car looked as if they would be all right. The response to steering seemed satisfactory after a period when Campbell had been complaining of oversteering, a too violent reaction to steering-wheel movement at higher speeds. The brakes and the safety parachute were functioning perfectly, and one of the biggest questions, the angle of incidence at which the car should run, seemed to have been settled.

For Norris this had been one of the queries about the car which only prolonged testing at high speeds could really answer. For this angle was crucial. From the side the car was shaped like the section of a wing. If the leading edge were raised a fraction too high when the car was travelling at speed, the car would begin to take off. If it were lowered too much, the air pressure on the top of the car would increase, and the load on the tyres become excessive. This could make *Bluebird* uncontrollable and send it right off course. Ideally the aerodynamic load on the car should stay zero so that the static weight of the car remained on the wheels throughout the speed range. The angle of incidence could be adjusted to allow for this.

'It's difficult to know what further advice to give you about the car,' said Norris, closing his file and leaning back in his chair. 'I can only tell you it *seems* all right. If the track was right and you felt like giving me half a dozen more really high speed runs I might be able to give you more definite answers. But the track's not right. I don't think it ever will be. If you go for the record it's going to be a hair's-breadth thing. It has to be your decision.'

Later that afternoon Leo Villa gave him much the same advice. 'We've checked the old car till there's nothing left to check. It's the worst bloody course I've ever seen for a car like this, but there you are, Skipper.'

But by now Campbell knew that whatever Norris said the decision had already been taken. Ready or unready, success or suicide, he would have to go now. He made the best of it, talking to his visitors, taking round the drinks, promising Lex Davison that he could drive the car once the record was won, and helping Florence put the champagne in the deep freeze. The deep freeze was very large and crammed with food. The champagne was the best Australian vintage that money could buy.

Perhaps it was the effect of a new audience, perhaps it was his way of relieving the tension, but at dinner he was on better form than he had been for weeks. He joked and laughed nervously, but those like Ken Norris and Leo Villa who understood his mood found it hard to laugh with him. Tonia was another one who seemed more withdrawn than usual. After dinner she sat for a while finishing off a pair of pale blue overalls for Campbell's teddy bear, Whoppit. Then she told him a letter had just arrived from his daughter Georgina, who was on holiday in Europe.

'She's staying at Como.'

'Como of all places,' replied Campbell. 'And I suppose you'll tell me next that she's staying at the Villa d'Este.'

'Of course.'

'My God,' said Campbell, putting his hand to his head in mock agony.

'That,' said someone, 'is what comes of bringing up a daughter to have expensive tastes.' And everyone laughed, Campbell as loud as anyone. But it was all unreal, feverish. It needed only the wrong word, the wrong remark, for all this bonhomie to collapse and the reality of Campbell's ordeal to reveal itself. One was grateful it did not happen.

Instead, Campbell stayed on at the homestead after dinner, smoked a pipe, put on his slippers, talked to Tonia, and behaved like the one thing in the world he was not—a comfortably domesticated middle-aged husband. And it was left to the rest of us to go to the nine o'clock meeting at the army camp to learn whatever arrangements were being made for the run the next morning.

Here the atmosphere was totally different from the genial cosiness which had seemed to protect Campbell up at the homestead. Several more reporters from the Sydney papers had joined Wally Parr, and all of them were out for news, digging away for what one of them kept calling 'the real inside story of this man Campbell'.

He was a reporter whose mere presence seemed to crystallise disaster out of the air, and the questions he asked caused the first rumours of Campbell's neck trouble to assume a new importance as one more major hazard to the attempt. As we walked to the army camp, he was trying hard to get Norris to talk. Norris did his best to be non-committal, but his flat, suddenly awkward voice was unable to conceal the anxiety he was feeling.

'He's all right, I tell you. I know him. I've seen all this before. He always gets keyed up before these things, but he's all right. You'll see tomorrow that he's all right.'

'But nerves are a terrible thing, Ken. They can make a man freeze up completely. Have you ever seen a man like that, Ken? Have you ever had nerves badly?'

'Look, I tell you the skipper's all right. I've seen him so bad with his back that he had to be lifted into that boat of his. Lifted bodily. Yet six times he went for that record and six times he got it.'

It was a dark, cool, dry night. There was a faint wind from the south-west. Rain had fallen again near Alice Springs, but the forecast for the following morning was good, and the cooks in the army camp were already hard at work cutting sandwiches for the hundred or so people expected on the lake at dawn next morning.

There must have been more than sixty people crammed into the big tent the army used as an orderly room for the meeting that night. More than ever now the circus seemed about to start. There was a smell of canvas, tobacco smoke, of dust, of sweat, of heavy clothing. The PRO for one of the cigarette companies was telling one of the specialist engineers in a loud voice, 'While you're here you can have all the cigarettes free that you can decently smoke.' It was that sort of evening.

The four stewards from the Confederation of Australian Motor-sports, who had flown in the previous afternoon, were there, further evidence for anyone who wanted it of how near we must now be to the record bid. They were there to enforce the rules of the Fédération Internationale d'Automobile. Without them no record could be officially recognised, and their presence lent an additional touch of seriousness to the meeting. These stewards were not just four ordinary Australians. They were the interna-tional jurisdiction. Here in this tent with its flickering lights and the dust underfoot and the nearest railhead forty miles away, they represented the world. On the following morning they would decide, on behalf of the rest of the globe, whether Campbell's performance entitled him to call himself the fastest man upon it.

I sat near two of them. One, a tall grey-haired man with a long beard and a kangaroo skin coat, looked like a younger brother of Father Time. The other, a heavy man with a large moustache, was wearing an army sweater and had a gold filling which half covered one of his front teeth.

They were serious men, and when I asked them about their duties they looked cautious as if guarding some inner truth which they were not over-anxious to reveal. The man in the beard explained impressively that the stewards 'exercised supreme juris-diction over the event'.

'We,' he went on, 'can stop it if we feel that the FIA regulations are being broken.'

But what were the FIA's regulations?

He shuffled papers in his hand and I caught sight of one headed 'Fédération Internationale d'Automobile'. It had a Paris address and was signed by an 'M. Schroeder, Gen. Sec.' Sensing my inter-est, he pushed them quickly into the pocket of the kangaroo coat.

'Safety matters,' he said. 'If spectators were getting too close and we thought this was an undue hazard to themselves or the driver…'

The man with the gold tooth joined in. 'We also have to make sure that his documentation is completely in order—that he has his racing permit from the RAC and his driving licence, and we issue a track licence of our own once we have checked the length of the measured mile and the measured kilometre and gone over the timing devices.

'As well as this,' he went on, 'we act as replenishment observers, checking that all the activities of the mechanics during the hour allowed them between runs are confined to minor things like tyres, oil and small adjustments. There must be no larger repairs to the car, otherwise a driver could go one way and then rebuild his car before driving back.'

His gold tooth suddenly twinkled as he laughed, and I asked him what he did for a living. 'Oh, this business here is quite honorary. I'm a bit of a car enthusiast in my spare time. I'm a company director.'

'Of what?'

'Well, off the record. Campbell would have forty fits if he knew. I'm a funeral director. Biggest in Melbourne.'

For some reason the formalities the stewards brought with them that evening were reassuring, confirming that all the anxiety and absurdity of the last few weeks at Lake Eyre were now going to take their place in an ordered, tradition-conscious world—a long-established, slightly dated world of wealthy European aristocrat automobilists, men with obscure titles and heavy overcoats roaring along oil-soaked, long-forgotten race tracks in Darracqs and Sunbeams and Hispano-Suizas in a splendour of dust and goggles and spoked wheels and external brake levers. Lake Eyre was simply the place where the motor car ended.

The seriousness of the stewards was echoed by Cliff Brebner when, as the man in charge of police arrangements for the next morning, he began explaining the rules that would govern all visitors to the lake.

'No vehicle will be allowed across the causeway on to the lake after zero six four five, repeat zero six four five hours tomorrow morning. No apologies will be allowed from anyone arriving after that. Anyone arriving later simply will not get on to the lake.'

And Evan Green, as one of the administrators of the run, gave the meeting its final macabre touch. 'We mean,' he announced, 'to have the car rolling by eight a.m. There will be one low speed run to test the extended track. Subsequent runs will take place at higher speeds. During all these runs the aircraft with the doctor aboard will be flying overhead. Should an emergency occur requiring the aircraft to land, only official police, army or project vehicles should go near the scene of the emergency. Provided everyone observes this, I think we are fully covered in case anything, repeat *anything*, goes wrong.'

But what could go wrong? It was not just the course that seemed the uncertain factor now. No one could tell what would happen the next time Campbell was alone in his cockpit with nothing to do except take the greatest risk of his life and put his foot down as hard as it would go.

As he went off to his bed at nine-thirty, there was not a man alive who would not have been afraid. What mattered was what he did with his fear, and what his fear did with him.

And there was to be yet another delay. During the night the wind increased, and by dawn it was reported to be blowing directly across the course at ten miles an hour, making any chance of holding *Bluebird* on its narrow course at four hundred clearly impossible. The run was again postponed.

It was as if the lake was waging a war on the nerves of Campbell, and the effect of one more postponement after he had keyed himself up to run that morning was perhaps the cruellest thing it had done to him yet.

Tonia was finding it more difficult now to hide her anxiety from him. He was depending on her to an extent she had never known before on a record attempt. When she had been with him on the boat records he had always made a great show of his independence so that she had felt little more than a spectator while the trials were on. Now it was different, and her very honesty made it hard for her to keep up the calm and unconcern he needed so badly from a woman.

She was worried about his neck, too. The effect of the prolonged tension was to make the muscles at the back seize up almost entirely, and for several days the displaced vertebrae had been giving him constant pain. Until now he had not spoken much about it—there had been enough depressing talk. But that Sunday morning the pain was so bad that he decided to do something about it.

Campbell has an almost mystical faith in anyone who has treated him successfully in the past, and now he decided that Mr Charles should make a special trip from Adelaide to treat him.

'He's a wizard, a bloody little wizard,' said Campbell, putting his hand behind his neck in the gesture most of us had grown familiar with. 'If I can only get him here he'll have me straightened out in no time. He's got a clinic in Adelaide. Charges a flat fee of ten shillings whatever he does for you. He's done more good with his two hands than most doctors with a hospital full of equipment.'

So little Mr Charles, former pharmacist, and qualified physiotherapist and osteopath, was flown into Muloorina by Peter Ahrens, who made a special flight to fetch him. For Campbell the pain in his neck was so bad that it seemed to swamp all his other troubles. When the plane landed at dusk with Mr Charles on board, it was as if the answer to all his troubles had arrived in one man.

Mr Charles had an air of knowing efficiency common to many of his calling. After a half-hour session with Campbell in his room he emerged to announce that yes, the neck had been bad. Three vertebrae had been seriously out of place, resulting in great pain and pressure on the nerve, but now they were back where they belonged and Campbell would have little to worry about.

He smiled shyly as he said this, blinking at us through large spectacles.

'I'll give him another massage before he goes off to sleep,' he said quietly to Tonia. 'You'll find that he'll rest well after that. The pain's gone already.'

He refused a drink, and said he would have to be flying back to Adelaide at first light. None of us could have guessed, looking at him, quite what repercussions his visit was to have for Campbell and the entire Bluebird Project.

13
First Attempt

The wind that caused such trouble on Sunday disappeared on Monday. Its going was as abrupt as its coming. Just before Monday's dawn the sky became still and full of stars. The first cocks were crowing and the run for which Campbell had waited nine long years was finally on. The first sign of it was when Leo Villa, who never slept, or at least never seemed to sleep, came with his torch to wake up his mechanics who were slumbering along the verandah.

'Go away, you old devil,' said a voice, and then one by one the rest of us woke and began struggling into clothes in the dark.

Campbell's greatest privilege that morning was to fly down to the lake just after seven instead of making the dawn exodus with the jeeps, the cars, the yellow Toyota fuelling wagons, the ambulances, the breakdown trucks, on their dusty convoy to the lake. Even so, it was too early for his liking. He hates the early morning, and looked tired and depressed as he climbed into the plane along with Tonia, Mason, MacLeonard, Dr Burke and a REME major he had promised a lift to the previous night.

No one asked about his neck, but he seemed to have developed fresh lines beneath his eyes overnight and had shaved badly. He was holding Tonia's hand very tightly.

Conversation was difficult, and the silence in that cramped little aircraft as it took off and circled up and away to the lake was an uncomfortable silence. The engines roared. Everyone stared ahead, rigidly minding his own business.

'Donald,' said a sudden voice from the other side of the cabin, 'would you mind counting from one to ten?' It was Dr Burke in combat suit, horn-rimmed spectacles and dark blue RAAF cap, who was sitting on the far side of the cabin.

'One-two-three-four-five-six-seven-eight-nine-ten,' replied Campbell, his lips scarcely moving, his voice already a voice from beyond the tomb.

'Good. *Good*.' Dr Burke's encouragement was affirmative, contrasting strangely with the apparent passivity of Campbell.

The lake was already coming into view below the aircraft. There was the line of the shore and the mud with its thin frosting of salt crinkling like scorched paintwork, the thicker salt beyond with its neater pattern of hexagonal cracks, and the pearl, rose, green, silver layers of the lake itself and the sun rising above the bright rim of the horizon.

'How are you feeling now, Donald?' came the voice of Dr Burke.

Campbell's reply was inaudible.

'Good, *good*,' said Dr Burke. 'Now Donald, would you mind just fixing this over your face.'

From somewhere the doctor had produced a small bag of opaque white polythene. A narrow plastic tube was attached to one end, leading to a small cylinder of carbon dioxide, and two elastic bands were fixed to the other. It fitted his face like something children wear at Christmas parties.

'That's right, Donald. That's right. The bands around the ears. Good. *Good*. Not too deeply, Donald. Just normally. Perfectly normal breathing please. Pretend it just isn't there.'

The rest of the passengers tried not to notice what was going on, as above the roar of the motors came the sudden hiss of carbon dioxide and Campbell began to inhale. As much of his face as was visible above the mask and the elastic bands was ashen.

'That will do, Donald.' The hissing stopped. 'Now you have nothing to worry about.'

On a record run success depends on a number of apparently minor factors. The effect of speed is to magnify. An ounce of salt on the rim of a wheel grows into a force that shakes a car to pieces at four hundred miles an hour. A bump in the track that a saloon car would fail to notice at forty miles an hour could deliver a car like *Bluebird* a blow of several tons when travelling at speed.

It is the same with the man who drives her—any weakness, any disequilibrium builds up, distorts, becomes one more source of danger. No one knew this better than Campbell. There was something contradictory in what was being demanded of him. With one part of him he had to forget all fear and commit himself unreservedly to the track, pushing his foot down the full four inches the throttle would travel. It had to be done like an act of faith or an act of love without thought for the consequence.

But with another part of him he had to hold himself in check even while he was risking everything. Never for a moment could he forget the knife-edge he was travelling. The slightest excess on his part, either of power or of steering, the slightest unpremeditated reaction could kill him on a track like this.

There was a certain amount that others could do for him. Leo Villa, for instance. In the two and a half hours the old man had been on the lake before Campbell's plane touched down, he and his assistants had been through the whole routine of double-checking the car for the last time—removing the wheels, testing the brakes and the suspension and the fuel pumps and the brake controls and the compressed air valves and the steering and the throttle.

Norris had his responsibilities as well. He had done his best to estimate the holding power of the salt and to work out the greatest kick it could bear from *Bluebird*'s wheels before the salt disintegrated and left them to spin out of control.

'You've a track length of thirteen point eight miles,' he said to Campbell, 'and we've set the engine to give you eighty-five per cent power. On that you should be able to take her straight up and still be accelerating as you go through the measured mile at something over four hundred.'

It sounded easy as he spoke, and Campbell nodded and said nothing. It was difficult to know how he was and whether he was up to it or not. He looked calm enough now, but then, with so many more people to watch him than there had been on any of his previous runs, no man as concerned with appearances as he was would have looked any other way. He had a few minutes to wait between talking to Norris and clambering into the cockpit and it was very still.

Until now everything had been exciting with a light-hearted excitement. Most of the people who had come for the weekend had managed to stay on—Mason and MacLeonard, the millionaire and his beautiful wife, the bony old man from Oodnadatta and his son.

These and many more had made the dawn journey to the lake and seen the sun come up, so close and huge over the horizon that it seemed one more trick of nature the lake put on to scare away its visitors. They had felt the night wind drop as the sun's rays grew stronger, and the two red and yellow Dunlop flags by the stewards' tent drooped in the stillness. They had seen the ambulances arrive, the big army wrecker with the skull and the bull's horns still on the radiator, and had watched Villa and his team making the last preparations for the car to run.

But now that Campbell had arrived and was standing alone by the car, the light-heartedness went. The talking stopped. There was a wait while the stewards made certain that Dr Burke was in the aircraft at the required spot above the course, and at eight-sixteen the cable from the booster motor was cast off, the stewards clicked their stop watches, and *Bluebird* roared away with one and only one intention—to go faster than Cobb and faster than Breedlove, to travel faster than any car of any type had travelled on land before.

At the south camp they had the radio receiver picking up Campbell from the car. As they waited for him to appear they heard the breathing, still heavy despite the carbon dioxide, and his voice, thick, slightly slurred by the opening and closing of the valves in the oxygen mask as he repeated the figures from the speedometer with the car accelerating towards the mile. Reception was clear, surprisingly clear, and the figures came between each breath— 'Two ninety—three hundred at the fourth mile—three twenty-three—thirty-five,' the voice counted its way forward.

'She's going through. She's going through. I'm holding her but she's through,' said the voice, and then there were no more words. The radio faded and the south camp had to wait, not knowing what had happened. Others were waiting along the track. Tonia in the Morris 1100 near the timekeepers' caravan saw the car streak past the tripods of the timing cameras trailing salt, saw the car seem to hesitate in the very middle of the mile then sway slightly to one side before sweeping on.

Lex Davison a little farther on saw it streak out of the mile still accelerating.

Norris and Villa inside one of the Valiants were already racing off along the service road to the southern camp to be there when Campbell opened the cockpit. 'You think he had enough power?' said Villa. 'On this track I couldn't risk him with more,' replied Norris.

It had been fast, very fast, but speeds of this level are hard to judge by eye, and no one knew whether he had done it or not.

Not even when the canopy lifted and Campbell sat there shaking his head did anyone know for sure. At first he seemed numbed.

'I'd say three eighty,' he said at last when Villa leaned over to ask him what he thought he had done. 'The wheels were going through the surface of the salt from the third mile on. It felt just as if the old car was ploughing its way through slush. Like a bloody great brake holding us back all the time.'

Evan Green came across from the control car where the radio

had just picked up the official timing from the timekeepers.

'Three eighty-nine, Donald.' It was the highest yet. It was five miles an hour short of the record.

He had failed, but he still seemed tantalisingly near to success. For the record is the average of the two journeys through the measured mile, and if only he could increase his speed a few miles an hour on the return run he could still have beaten Cobb.

The lines, the anxiety, were back in Campbell's face, and as he sat there on the edge of the cockpit it was as if the realisation of what he had to do was seeping into him a little at a time.

'Cobb made only three seventy-eight on one of his runs for the record,' said Evan Green.

'How fast would I need to go to make it on this next run?' said Campbell, looking hard at Norris.

'Four twenty-seven,' he replied. And as he spoke we all knew that such a speed was possible and yet impossible. It was possible if the power was increased. There was another fifteen per cent the turbine could give, and fifteen per cent should easily be enough to carry the car through that extra twenty miles an hour he needed. But this would be suicide if the track really was collapsing now, if the car had been on the very edge of disaster on its first run, and Campbell had just managed to pull it through.

Once again we were back with the question which no one could answer. The question of how much risk a record breaker should be asked to take or allowed to take.

It was a crucial moment. Campbell was still keyed up enough to have put his foot down, and if Leo Villa or Norris had taken the responsibility of nodding and saying, 'give her maximum power' he would have agreed then and might have just got away with it. He might just have been able to hold the car on its narrow course, just have stopped the wheels spinning at the intersection of the old main track where for four hundred yards the surface of the salt was at its wettest and softest. He might even have scraped the extra twenty miles an hour he needed and become world champion that morning.

Or he might have killed himself.

But Leo Villa and Norris kept quiet. This was not their decision any more. It was up to Campbell.

The turn-round team was hard at work now. The car was already jacked up on its rams, the covers off the wheel fairings, the mechanics in their overalls changing wheels, checking oil, gear-box temperatures, radio, oblivious of the decision Campbell was having to make.

'It's the salt again, Unc,' he said suddenly. 'That bloody salt. I'm digging great furrows in it.' He paused, turned away, and for a moment it seemed as if he knew that talking about the salt at this stage was useless. Either he went for the record or he called it off. That was all he had to decide, and just then it looked as though he was going to shut his mind to everything except getting back into the cockpit and calling for the power he needed and putting his foot down.

'How deep d'you think the ruts were, Skipper?' asked Villa.

'I don't know. All I know is that every so often there was a surge forward as if the car was in water, and then it would be held back again when the wheels went in the ruts. Why don't we go and have a quick look? See just how much damage we've done. Have to be quick, mind you, but we must see how bad those ruts really are.'

It was a mistake, of course. In every way it was a mistake. No one in the middle of risking his neck should pause and try to assess the danger all over again. He had started the morning by forcing shut his mind against the probability of his death. Now he was allowing it to open again. And it looked bad to have a world contender squandering so many of those bare sixty minutes he possessed for his two runs in inspecting the track.

Nevertheless he went, in the grey, lake-stained Valiant, with Ken Norris driving and Leo Villa beside him and Evan Green in the back seat. And when he came to the sixth mile of the course where the car had been under full power and had burned into the salt in two long straight scars that stretched from horizon to horizon, he stopped the car and got out and took his silver lighter to measure the depth of the ruts and said, 'For crying out loud, Unc, look at it. Look what the power does to it. We've not a hope in hell.'

'We shouldn't have brought him here,' said Evan Green to Norris. 'He shouldn't have had the sight of this to worry him on top of everything else.'

They climbed back into the Valiant and drove on to the centre of the measured mile itself. The performance was repeated with Campbell and Leo Villa probing the salt and standing silent, white-faced both of them in the middle of that glaring emptiness.

By now all the calm, all the resolution which Campbell had been so carefully guarding all morning had gone. He was beginning to talk too much and with him this is always a bad sign.

'Look at it. What a hope we've got. Forget it. Let's all forget the whole silly damned business.' He ground his heel furiously into the salt making a dent an inch deep with water at the bottom. 'this course will never get dry. There's a jinx on it. It's this lake, this bloody lake. It's out to get me and this morning it nearly succeeded. Look up there.' And he pointed to the south end of the track, and everyone could see the way the deep tram-lines of his tracks veered right away from the straight blue dye line marking dead centre until they were a few feet from the rough, ungraded surface of the rest of the lake. It was only near the end of the measured mile that the tracks got back again to the guide line.

'That's what happened when I nearly lost her. You get a swerve like that and you smash the whole thing.'

His left hand was massaging the back of his neck again. 'That's what happens, isn't it, Ken? You end up smashing the whole damned thing. I tell you, Ken, this scares me. It scares me. It scares me stiff.'

And it scared the rest of them too—that was the trouble. It convinced them that if they allowed him to go ahead and push full power through a course in this state they would spend the rest of their lives with his death on their consciences. Nobody spoke on the journey back to the south camp where *Bluebird* had already been waiting—checked, refuelled and ready to drive, for more than twenty minutes.

Everyone was on edge by now and no one, not even Campbell, knew what was to be done. For him the situation was intolerable. He had come to the lake that morning prepared for anything. At the start of that first run he had made himself believe that it could be done. He had shut his mind to the odds against him, to his doubts about himself, to all those nameless fears of something against him which would always prevent him getting the record on Lake Eyre.

But now that he had seen the evidence for himself it was hard to avoid the truth. The lake was against him, and however many charms he carried on his key ring, however carefully he avoided green or Fridays or spilling salt, he would end up killing himself if he pushed his luck any further.

For the people who were waiting, the issue was nothing like so clear. All they knew was that the wind was rising, the salt getting wetter, the minutes ticking past. None of them knew what Campbell knew or had to fear what he feared.

He had got to within five miles of the record on one run and now, instead of turning round and going back those few miles an hour faster to beat Cobb, he was sitting on the step of the Valiant, rubbing his neck and showing no signs of moving.

His wife was the only person who really knew what he was up against. She knew that his fear was no ordinary fear. She knew how involved was the battle he was fighting with himself. She knew about his superstition. She understood everything that was at stake for him now, and how the very burden of all this was making his risk so much heavier than it looked.

And because she understood, there was nothing she could do, except sit and wait in one of the cars and show him, just by being there, that she was not anxious and that he could do what he had to.

'I don't know what your intentions are, Mr Campbell, but your hour's nearly up. Unofficially I would say that you have seven minutes left, but I emphasise it's unofficial.'

This was one of the stewards, and his formality came as a reminder that the attempt was still on, that something was still expected of him. It produced a sudden effect from Campbell, the sort of desperate, emotional reflex of which he was always capable.

'Ken!' he shouted. 'Ken. Let's get it done. Increase the power. I'm taking her back. Quick as we can.' Suddenly he was away from the car, running towards *Bluebird*, and everyone started scurrying after him to get him away while there was still time. His shoes, his helmet, Whoppit the bear, were rushed to the cockpit. The booster motor whined, the timekeepers were informed he was on his way, and he roared off with an extra five per cent of power.

It was partly for his own sake that he went. He had to prove that he could still do it. It was partly for the others. He had to show them he had not lost his nerve. It was brave and it was desperate, but it was quite pointless. He made a speed of just over three sixty and then hit an exceptionally wet patch of salt and felt *Bluebird* going out of control. He nearly lost her then and had to ease her down before the mile. And even if he had not, even if he had added the twenty miles an hour he needed to his previous speed, he still would not have got his record.

For the steward had been right to emphasise the unofficial nature of those seven minutes he had told Campbell he still possessed. When the timekeepers checked *Bluebird*'s second run through the measured mile they found he was already eight and a half minutes over the hour. He had been outside it even when he stepped into the cockpit.

14
Götterdämmerung

'There'll be trouble now,' said Tonia. 'I know all the signs. I've never seen him as patient as he's been here at Lake Eyre. But he's not a patient man, and no one can go on for ever taking disappointments like he had this morning.'

She spoke with detachment and a certain pride now as if describing some phenomenon of nature over which she had no control. Round her neck she wore a small golden ram's horn on a long thin chain, which she twisted between her fingers as she talked. 'There's a devil in him, you know. It's what drives him on. Usually he keeps it hidden, but whenever he feels cheated of anything it breaks out. He's feeling cheated now. You saw the way he went when the stewards asked him all those questions after the run. That man with the long whiskers and the leather coat asking him why he started a few minutes late and why there had been a delay between the two runs. D'you think that Donald would normally put up with that sort of thing? But you noticed how he went, very quiet, very British. That's always a bad sign with him.'

Since the failure of the record bid that morning the one topic of conversation had been what Campbell would do now, for with this unpredictable, chameleon-like man the next move was always enigmatic, and failure seemed to have inspired him with fresh energy.

At first it looked as if he was going to postpone everything until September. He had come to the homestead, refused lunch and sat at the dining-room table discussing the chances of reassembling his specialist engineers in two or three months' time when the lake had hardened. 'This car of yours is wonderful, Ken old boy. This morning it did far more than any of us had a right to expect. But if we go on we're just going to smash it up. And at this stage of the game that's the one thing I'm not prepared to do, even if it means all the expense and disappointment of waiting until September.'

'But have you any certainty that conditions will be any better in September than they are now?' asked Norris wearily.

'Ask old Elliott here. He's the expert on the lake. What's it going to be like here in September, Elliot—for the rain statistics don't help us here at all?'

The old man had been concentrating on his bread and cheese. At Campbell's question he laid down his knife and looked very wise.

'Well, Don, could come good.' He munched thoughtfully. 'Could go crook on you too. Hard to tell. All depends when it rains. From now on's the time we hope for it. If we don't have a couple of inches between now and September things'll be looking pretty rough for me'n the sheep.'

'What about some other part of the lake then, Elliot? It's a big place. D'you know of anywhere at all now where we could get a stretch of hard salt free of islands?'

'Well, there's Jackboot Bay, fifty mile or so to the west. I flew over it a month or two back and the salt looked hard from the air. It might suit you.'

'But what good's that?' said Norris. 'We've thought of Jackboot Bay before, but we'd never get *Bluebird* on to it. There's no road. There's no causeway on to the salt. It would take another month or so to get established there, even if the salt was any good.'

'Well we can't just sit around talking. At least we can go and see. Will you come with me, Elliot, and show me the place you're thinking of?'

Campbell already had his khaki haversack over his shoulder and was drumming impatiently on the table with his lighter. 'We'll take the Aero Commander,' he added.

'Sure, Don. Let me finish my tea and I'll come. If I can help you get that record now I'm game for anything.'

Once the plane had taken off, the recriminations started.

One by one the visitors had left. MacLeonard of Ampol had been the first to go. 'Sorry I can't stay,' he said as he climbed aboard the company plane, his dispatch case bloated with papers, 'but our people have just struck oil in Western Australia. We've been looking for it for fifteen years. Now it seems we might have it at last, and they need me back in Sydney.'

The millionaire and his beautiful wife were the next to go. They flew off from Muloorina in a small sleek yellow monoplane with two very powerful engines which blew the dust up from the runway into a mournful red cloud which hung in the air some time, signalling their departure.

Florence left before lunch in the charter plane she booked to take her to Adelaide. She left behind the six bottles of Great Western champagne, unconsumed in the deep freeze. 'It's good champagne,' she shouted. 'I'll be back to drink it with you. Make sure you keep it cool everyone.'

All that afternoon there were rumours about the stewards.

'I don't understand what they're up to,' said Wally Parr, 'but there's something cooking. They won't say anything to the press and they had a long session with Andrew Mustard. They were questioning Norris this morning too, you know. When the second run was over and they'd had a word with Donald, they asked Ken to stay behind and looked at the track with him. They all looked grim. There's someone else too they seem very interested in.'

'Who's that?'

'Campbell's doctor friend. He's up at their tent in the army camp now.'

I left Parr and walked towards the creek. The water was a greenish yellow and the high soda content made it useless for irrigation. The mud along the banks where the cattle had been was frosted with small white crystals.

A late afternoon wind had begun. Geese and ibis with their large delicate fan-shaped wings were flying in to roost, and behind them followed the storm clouds like range upon range of black mountains driven down from the north.

Nearer the homestead the shores of the creek joined the dumping ground for the sheep station, and I was soon picking my way through broken bottles, whisky crates, sheep skeletons, sacks, old boots hidden among the wattle bushes. Near a windowless car crows were pecking at the bodies of two small grey kangaroos. They lay neatly side by side like a freshly murdered married couple.

The birds shuffled as I approached then flew languidly away, cawing. Then a small boy with fair hair rode up on a bicycle with a pair of rusty rabbit traps dangling from the handlebars. I recognised him as one of Elliot's grandsons.

He took no notice of me, got off the bicycle, and then started burying the two traps in the sand a few inches from the corpses. He worked deftly, frowning slightly as he concentrated on setting the jaws with a hair trigger and then trickling dust across the platform of each trap and smoothing the sand round them until they were invisible.

'Why do you do that?' I asked.

'For the crows,' he said.

'Why?'

'Don't know. We just catch 'em, m'cousin and me. Stupid buggers, crows.'

It was some time after five when I returned to the homestead. The Aero Commander was back already and Campbell was in the sitting room with Ken Norris. His face was slightly flushed and he looked excited.

'Here,' he said. 'D'you want to hear something to make you laugh, something really funny?' He smiled that forced, small boy's smile of his. His hair was rumpled. The collar of his blue shirt had got tucked beneath the neck of his darker blue sweater, revealing the nylon cord of the gold St Christopher medal his father gave him.

'D'you know what they've done—the stewards and our good doctor? They've decided to take exception to the fact that I invited my friend Mr Charles to come and take a look at my neck. They say it gives them grave doubts about the state of my health and fitness to drive. And they're coming to deliver an ultimatum about it at six-thirty this evening. Funny, isn't it. Really funny. First this morning, now this.'

He paced across the room and back. He was wearing his old blue slippers. The leather was slightly scuffed and the backs broken down.

Ken Norris looked tired and worried. There was no further news about his wife, but he had been counting on the record being won that morning so he could fly back to Sydney with MacLeonard.

'I don't understand, Don,' he said. 'I just don't understand what everyone's up to.'

'I do,' said Campbell. 'All too well I do.'

'Take it easy, Don,' said Norris. 'I know how you feel. After what you went through this morning it's beyond me how anyone can do this to you. But don't do anything silly. You've more at stake than anyone. For God's sake be careful.'

'Ken, old scout, I've been careful too long. That's been my trouble.'

'What are you going to do then?'

'I've asked the press to be present this evening when the stewards make their bloody announcement. Every word they say is going to be on the record.'

He saw the expression on Norris's face. 'Don't look so worried, Ken. It doesn't suit you. The time's come for a showdown, that's all.'

It was an uncomfortable occasion as we waited for the stewards in the Prices' sitting room. Campbell sat at the head of the room in the large wooden armchair from the dining room, his back to the empty fireplace. On his left were Evan Green and Dick Mason of Ampol, who had decided not to travel back with his boss to Sydney. Wally Parr was there, and Ken Norris was next to him. We sat in silence.

At six-thirty on the dot a car drew up outside and headlights glared through the badly cracked frosted glass of Elliot Price's front door. A car door slammed, and Campbell drew himself up in his chair and breathed so deeply that the tendons on his neck showed. He was tense and pale.

The first of the stewards to enter was the beared orchardist in the kangaroo-skin coat. He was followed by the gold-toothed Melbourne undertaker and Andrew Mustard.

'Good evening, gentlemen,' said Campbell. 'And what can I do for you?'

The undertaker was holding a piece of thin typing paper headed 'Notice from Stewards to Donald Campbell' and I caught sight of their signatures at the bottom in quavering blue biro.

'We have something we would like to communicate to you,' said the orchardist, tugging at his beard.

'Please be seated, gentlemen,' said Campbell. 'And just one thing before we start. I would like to remind you that the press is present. Everything we say here tonight is going to be very much on the record and you continue at your peril.'

He sat bolt upright, chin drawn in, hands gripping the side of the chair. The two stewards sat and looked equally uncomfortable.

'We would request,' said the undertaker, 'that we have a private audience.'

'Gentlemen, I am not disposed to giving private audiences. I repeat, anything that is said must be said in public.' And to complete the formalities Campbell went round the room introducing us all one by one—'Mr Walter Parr, representing the Australian Associated Press, Mr Dick Mason of Ampol, and Mr Andrew Mustard. Whom do you represent, Mr Mustard?'

'I am here at the request of the stewards,' said Mustard, looking understandably puzzled, 'and as reserve driver of *Bluebird*.'

'And may I make myself plain. You are relieved of your duties as reserve driver and discharged from my employ, effective immediately.'

Before Mustard could reply the undertaker had stepped forward to deliver his piece. He read from the typewritten paper and invested his words with rich legality like a summons read before a court.

'Notice from the Stewards to Mr Donald Campbell.' He cleared his throat. 'It has been brought to our notice that on May the twenty-sixth one or more osteopaths were brought to Muloorina to treat Mr Donald Campbell for complaints which were not disclosed to our medical officer, Flight Lieutenant Burke, and which may endanger his ability to handle *Bluebird* at high speeds. We therefore deem it prudent and proper under Rule NCR 122 to insist that Mr Donald Campbell have a medical examination before being allowed to continue driving.'

He finished and sat down heavily on the sofa, wiping his moustache with a large handkerchief. There was silence in the room. Campbell spoke.

'When I was informed that you two gentlemen were coming here to see me this evening I took the liberty of putting a call through to your general secretary in Melbourne, Mr Don Thompson. I suggest that you now telephone him straight away for yourselves and read this message over to him. The telephone is here.'

This suggestion caught the stewards unprepared. Whatever reception they had been expecting, it had clearly been nothing like this public counter-attack.

'Very well then,' said the undertaker, and put the call through to Melbourne.

For a minute or so he listened attentively to what the fifteen-hundred-mile-distant Mr Thompson had to say.

'Now just hear me a minute, Mr Thompson,' he said. 'I'd like to ready over to you Rule 122, just as it is in the book.' He repeated the words about the stewards having the power to insist on a medical examination for any contender in a record attempt. 'And I'd like to emphasise the last line,' he said. '"No appeal shall lie against this decision of the stewards." You hear that, Mr Thompson? If you want to fly over here you damn well can. And I may add that I strongly object to Mr Donald Campbell coming to you over our heads.

'Now Mr Thompson, I'm not standing for that from any competitor whether his standing is as high as his or not.

'We don't make statements to the press—you ought to know that.'

'I cannot comment on that because there are gentlemen of the press here at the moment taking down every word of this conversation.'

There was a long pause then. Presumably Mr Thompson at Melbourne was having his say. The rest of us kept silent, watching the uncomfortable undertaker and wondering what he would do next.

'Mr Thompson,' he said. 'I have Ken Archibald, the senior steward, here with me and I'd like him to hear what you are saying. Would you mind repeating those last few words while we share the telephone?'

Unfortunately for the two stewards a telephone is not an object two grown men can share with decorum, especially when one is exceptionally tall and bearded and the other is portly with a very large moustache. But they did their best. They stood together as if practising a tango, cheek to cheek with only the earpiece of the telephone between them. First one then the other would speak.

'You'd better come over and see for yourself,' said the orchardist.

'Mr Thompson,' said the undertaker. 'Will you please take a plane and get to South Australia straight away?'

'We don't intend to resign our stewardship. That's flat.'

'Our position is impossible.'

'Our position is untenable.'

'You're just not in possession of the facts. This is absolutely necessary. We have expert opinion.'

'This order is a request for a medical examination. We're just asking him to be examined.'

'But why replace two stewards who are simply trying to do their jobs?'

'How do you know, sir? What about the danger to the spectators and the timekeepers?'

'That would be very comforting to their widows.'

'If you want to replace us that's okay by me.'

'The name is Geoffrey.'

'I cannot speak to you any further without becoming very annoyed and agitated.'

With this the conversation ended, and without another word to us the two of them swept out with deathly dignity.

Campbell ignored the whole incident. 'The first thing I would like to clear up, gentlemen, is that I asked a very good friend, a physiotherapist mark you, not a chiropractor, to visit me because of some pain I have been having recently in my neck. The second matter is that I have requested Dunlops for your recall, Mr Mustard, sir.'

'That,' replied Mustard, *sotto voce*, face the palest pink above orange whiskers, 'will not be necessary. My own direct association with Dunlops terminated some while ago.'

'Very well. You will be paid through my lawyers.'

'And I take it I am at liberty to withdraw my personnel and equipment from the project?'

'Certainly.'

Campbell paused and looked around the silent room. 'Today has seen the conditions the car has had to battle with,' he said. 'It is a tribute to Ken Norris's design and to British industry that

Bluebird achieved what she did. I would also like to pay a tribute to the Commonwealth for all the help the project has had.

'As to the unfortunate references to my fitness, I would like to say that together, Leo, Ken and I hold more records than any other team in the world, past or present, with the sole exception of my father's. I hold an official licence from the FIA. Also civilian air pilot's licences from England, America and Australia. All involved stringent medical examinations—the last in February 1964.'

He stopped. The meeting was over, but Andrew Mustard chose to stay a moment longer.

'This afternoon, sir, I asked you if you were chucking the rag in. I would like to ask you the same question again. Are you?'

Campbell glared at him, and when he spoke his voice was thick with anger.

'Despite aspersions by poor unfortunate individuals, we don't chuck the rag in. Good night.'

A dazed silence followed Mustard's departure. It took time for the full implication of these last few minutes to sink in. Then one by one we realised we had probably been listening to the end of the *Bluebird* Project. The fuse was lit now. It would take only a little time for the explosion. Within a few hours it would be front-page news in Sydney and Adelaide—the row with the stewards, the break with Mustard, the doubts cast on Campbell's fitness to drive.

In one disastrous day Campbell would have lost nearly everything he possessed—his track, his official authority to get a record—and he would be at the centre of a full-scale controversy which would split the camp wide open and have to be conducted in public. No one, not even he, could hope to survive it.

He must have realised this too. Just as we were about to leave he spoke to Parr, and for the first time that evening there was a note of caution in his voice.

'Wally, old boy. Just one thing before you go.' He groped uncertainly for the right phrase. 'Perhaps—if you don't mind—it might be best for the project if we treated all this as off the record.'

Parr paused a moment as he was putting his notebook away and there was an uncomfortable silence. It was an unforgivable request to make of any reporter. When he answered he spoke very slowly.

'Very well, Donald. Very well. Although I feel as if I had just been used as a club to beat a lot of people over the head with.'

If *Bluebird* was to survive now, someone had to act as mediator, and it was Norris, sane, worried Ken Norris, who took charge. The first person he enlisted was Evan Green. 'Evan,' he said, 'we must stop this going any further. Enough damage has been done already. If we want to keep the project together we've got to act and act fast.

'First priority is to look after Don and you're the man to do it. He trusts you and will do what you say. Keep him away from the press and away from the stewards. Explain what's happened to Tonia. He needs sleep desperately. I know him when he's like this. I saw it coming and should have done something about it earlier. It was the strain of this morning's run with the disappointment and frustration on top of everything else. It all boiled up. It's his way of letting off steam. Just get him to bed now and he'll be right as rain tomorrow.'

'I'll do my best,' said Green. 'But where are you going? What's your next move?'

Norris paused at the verandah door and grinned. 'I'm going to see Andrew Mustard first and then those stewards. It's in nobody's interests to bust everything up at this stage. I'll get Don to withdraw his dismissal of old Andrew. Then I'm going to calm the stewards down if I can.'

'I wish you luck,' said Green.

'I'll need it. Just look after Don. He's been pushed a bit too far today.'

One of the grey Valiants was standing outside the homestead. Norris got in and started the engine.

'I'll let you know how I get on,' he shouted, and drove off into the darkness in the direction of the army camp.

'It was a great story,' said Parr mournfully.

'It was,' I replied. 'Why did you kill it? You didn't have to. I can't think of many reporters who would have acted as nobly as you did.'

'It wasn't being noble,' he said as he finished his beer. He wiped his mouth with the back of his hand. 'It was sentimentality. Sheer sentimentality. I must be getting old. You see, I like the man. At times there's a wonderful air of innocence about him. And I don't want to see him destroy himself, though he seemed hell-bent on it this evening.'

'What will happen if the story does get out?'

'It'll be the last of Campbell—at Lake Eyre at any rate. It will be the biggest row of his career. There will be an investigation, and whatever the rights and wrongs of the case, he can't possibly afford that sort of thing now. He'll lose his specialist engineers, and the government will probably pull out.'

'But *will* it happen, do you think?'

'Probably. I'm not the only pressman here now, you know. Peter Michelmore's covering it for the *Adelaide Advertiser*, and his stuff's being syndicated to London. He's only got to persuade Mustard or one of the stewards to talk and there's the whole story ready made. I expect things have gone too far to be patched up now.'

Peter Michelmore was tall and tough and charming. More important, he was a freelance who was paid by results. When he called at the homestead within an hour of Campbell's meeting, he knew what he wanted.

Evan Green tried coping with him on the lines Norris suggested, but it was difficult. He stood awkwardly in the doorway of the homestead as if guarding everything that lay beyond, and Michelmore, fair-haired, decisive with notebook and neatly tailored gaberdine golf jacket, had to ask his questions from outside.

'Evan, there's a lot of talk around the camp about a break between Donald and the stewards and Andrew Mustard. I'd like to know how much truth there is in it.'

'No comment at this stage, Peter. Sorry.'

'Very well then. I'm formally asking you for an interview with Campbell.'

'Sorry. That'll have to wait until tomorrow. Don's very tired after the strain of this morning's run and is in bed asleep.'

'That makes it very hard for me if I'm going to get the story straight. Is there nothing at all you can tell me?'

Green shifted his weight from one foot to the other. 'Nothing at all. Donald's very tired and I've no intention of disturbing him tonight.'

So the evening ended and the future of the Bluebird Project was still in the balance. Campbell slept peacefully. The stars were very bright and there was a cold wind from the north.

Norris's grey Valiant was parked up at the army camp until nearly midnight. Michelmore was busy too, and it was very late before he had seen all the people he needed, typed his story, and telephoned it over for the morning editions. And in the army tent someone got drunk and threw a can-full of Southwark Bitter into the sad Irish face of Dr Burke. But for the firmness and tact of Superintendent Brebner, there might have been quite a fight of it.

15
Full Throttle...

'Well?' said Evan Green.

'Keep your fingers crossed,' said Norris.

'Did you see the stewards?'

'Yes. And Andrew Mustard. He's coming at nine for a meeting with Donald.'

'Are we going to get away with it?'

'We might. No one wants direct responsibility for wrecking the project, and there are a lot of second thoughts about what was said and done last night. Let's hope a good night's sleep has done its work.'

'What about the press?'

'Some of the story got out, but it's not as bad as it might have been. The Adelaide headlines this morning are "Rumours of Split in Campbell Camp". If that's the lot we can survive.'

'What about your wife? Any news?'

'Nothing. I must get home soon. At the moment I'm feeling a bit too responsible for everyone.'

It was eight o'clock the following morning, and the appearance of the two men on the verandah of the homestead was the first sign of life in the camp. The day seemed reluctant to begin. The crows were cawing from the cattle pens and the sun had risen coldly in the east. Now that the record bid had lost its way, Muloorina had lapsed back to its normal tempo with the wind-pump clanking by the creek, the geese nesting among the reeds, the dogs scavenging behind the slaughter-house.

'We'd better get some breakfast,' said Green.

'I've had mine,' replied Norris.

Somehow the news that Andrew Mustard was coming got round the camp, and by nine everyone was outside the homestead to watch him arrive. It was odd. Muloorina had seen nothing like it before with these small, silent knots of people standing waiting for something to happen—the cameramen in one group, the specialist engineers in another, the mechanics and drivers and military police in yet another. From the homestead they looked ominous, like people waiting for a great man to die or a government to fall.

They heard the clock on the Prices' mantelpiece strike nine—a measured, solemn sound—and as it finished the big blue Humber drove up with Mustard at the wheel.

Still no one spoke. No one said, 'Good morning, Andrew.' They just watched as he got out of the car and strode, beard in air, through the fly-proof door with the notice 'Do *Not* Slam' on it. It slammed behind him.

Norris and Evan Green followed him into the sitting room where Campbell had been waiting for some time. There was no sign of the stewards.

Outside the people stayed on. The day became warmer. The crows fell silent. Some of the watchers wandered off for beer. At ten-thirty one of Elliot's grandsons came out of the homestead and walked towards the shearing shed.

'What are they doing in there?' someone asked him.

'Talking.'

'Still?'

The boy nodded.

'What's that you've got inside your shirt?' one of the cameramen asked.

'Nothing.'

'But I saw something moving.'

The boy scuffed in the dust and carefully regarded his shoes.

'It's me dragon. I shouldn't get too near. He'll bite you.'

'Can't we see it?' asked the cameraman politely.

The boy examined his shoes a while longer. 'All right. I'll put him on the log by the petrol pump. He likes it there. But watch out. He'll kill anyone he doesn't know.'

Quite a crowd had collected round the boy now, and they followed him over to the log. He reached inside his shirt, and after fumbling a moment brought out a fat brown lizard fourteen inches long with a body as thick as a man's wrist. It looked prehistoric. Its scales shone. When it blinked in the strong sunlight a milk-white eyelid swivelled across a beady black eye.

'He knows me,' said the boy, tickling the scaly head with a grimy forefinger. The animal yawned obligingly, revealing a mouth like a miniature man-trap lined with hard red flesh. 'Dragons is real dangerous,' he said.

The lizard stayed motionless on its log, and the cameramen decided to film it for want of anything better. They took a lot of trouble, but the small boy remained unimpressed.

It was eleven before there was any further sign of life from the homestead. Evan Green came out, sheet of paper in hand, look of troubled sincerity on his face.

'The dispute, gentlemen, has been settled.' Campbell's way of speaking was contagious. 'The next high speed run will take place on Thursday. After yesterday's run there are four ruts eight miles long to be filled in with salt, then the course will be left to harden. This will take a minimum of three days. Frankly, gentlemen, we are on a knife edge now. *Bluebird* was designed for . . . '

'Excuse me, Evan,' said Michelmore, butting in suddenly. 'What about the trouble between Campbell and Andrew Mustard? Is Mustard still working for him or not?'

'His position is what it always has been.'

'Good. And the stewards. Has that been cleared up too?'

'Off the record, Peter, I think I can put you in the picture. You will appreciate . . .'

'I appreciate that I am here to report a story for a newspaper. Too much has been said off the record already. All I want to know is what I can print.'

Green looked sad.

'Very well, Peter. All I can say is that we anticipate no major problems over the stewards either.'

The terms of the armistice Ken Norris worked out between Campbell, Mustard and the stewards were to remain obscure. Mustard assured Campbell that he had had nothing to do with the stewards' action. He returned to his old job. The stewards were not replaced. They remained in the chilly dignity of self-imposed exile up at the army camp and Parr said that when Campbell was ready for his next bid a new doctor would be brought in to examine him. Once this was done there could be no further objections. The crisis, it seemed, was over.

But Campbell seemed despondent about his chances. At dinner that Tuesday he ate little, said little. Dick Mason of Ampol was sitting on his left and did most of the talking. He is a kindly, good-looking man and he was doing his best to be helpful, but everything he suggested seemed to add to the gloom.

'In Hong Kong our company has the agency for some stuff called Kompak. It's a chemical they spray on to stabilise the surface of dirt roads. I don't see why it shouldn't work on salt. We could always give it a try. Perhaps I'll have some flown up.'

Campbell said nothing and pushed away his plate with most of his steak uneaten.

'And have you thought of some sort of matting? If you could get enough of it and lay it along the course that might do the trick. But there'd be the difficulty of fastening it down, I suppose.'

'Or how's about the Nullarbor Plain,' he said. 'It looks pretty flat when you go across it on the train from Adelaide to Perth.

There's seven hundred miles of it. You ought to be able to find just fifteen that would take *Bluebird*.'

'Old chum,' said Campbell. 'I'm afraid this is all a bit late in the day for us. From now on it's Lake Eyre or nothing.'

'The best hotel in the south of France? You mean where would I stay, old boy? Money no object?'

Campbell pondered. A wintry smile broke across his face. 'La Réserve, I suppose. La Réserve at Beaulieu not far from Nice.'

He rubbed his stomach and leaned back in his chair. 'I've had some times there in the past like nobody's business. Wonderful food. Gorgeous girls. Back around 1955 in the early days of the water speed record. That really was the life.'

The thought revived old dreams, half-forgotten memories of the time he had been the young record breaker, the *wunderkind*— when the challenge of a new record had been part of the happiest years of his life. It was hard to believe it had all gone wrong. Perhaps it could still be recovered. Perhaps the old days were not so far away as they seemed.

'If we could only get away with it this time, that's where you'd find me. They do wonderful *moules* in the restaurant there. I love seafood. Just think. The only thing standing between me and those damned mussels is twenty miles an hour on the salt of Lake Eyre. But I don't see myself tasting them this year. I just don't see it.'

Thursday's run took place according to plan. Campbell had been examined by a regular air force doctor and found perfectly fit and the stewards raised no objections after this. But it was hopeless from the start. A six-mile-an-hour wind was blowing across the track at eight a.m. It increased as the morning went on, and when Campbell took *Bluebird* up to three hundred miles an hour at nine-thirty, he reported that it was almost impossible to keep her straight.

It was the worst defeat so far. It seemed as if all the efforts and anxieties of the last few days to keep the project going had been wasted after all. Campbell had survived so much that he deserved something better. But the life had gone out of everything, and even the car looked tired. When the run was over, he went off on his own without talking to a soul.

He walked towards the hangar where he had left his haversack and his new anorak. His shoulders were hunched, his head down, and the whole idea of the record suddenly seemed part of the private obsession of a very lonely man. When he had been winning, when the speed had been climbing and there was still optimism in the air, the Bluebird Project had been something everyone wanted to share, but now in defeat *Bluebird* was his alone. Failure made it belong to him in a way success never could have done.

The sun was hot but the wind was gusting across the lake, flapping the canvas sides of the hangar, blowing Campbell's hair. He stood with his hands in his pockets, back to us all, staring away to an empty horizon. I remembered what he told me not long after I arrived at Lake Eyre when he had just finished showing me the car and the organisation.

'You know why I do all this?' he had asked. 'Conceit—no other reason when you boil it all down. The conceit of believing that this is something I can do better than anyone else in the world. I suppose it's the same with artists or actors or politicians. Everyone likes to think that they're unique. This is my way of proving it.'

And as he stood there by the hangar so completely cut off from the rest of us I realised that he would keep going—that whatever the odds, whatever the hopelessness, he would never give in. This was not merely because he was brave. Brave men will surrender when courage becomes useless. It was his inability ever to accept that he was commonplace like the rest of us. And the more he lost heart, the stronger would be his resolve. For despair is commonplace, and only success would ever convince him that he was still unique.

After that Thursday, time slowed down. It was Campbell against the rest of us now.

'It's impossible,' said Parr. 'He's punch-drunk. He can't get the record and he can't give up. It's absurd. What hope's he got now?'

'None at all, I should think. But you're dealing with an unusual man here. He doesn't need hope. He just waits. He's done it before with the boat.'

'But the boat was different. It didn't have all this great organisation. If he wants to wait much longer, he'll soon be here on his own. Brebner's men have itchy feet. So have the track staff. The specialist engineers are getting orders from their firms in England to go home, and Norris is already staying on borrowed time. It can't last much longer.'

But it did. The attempt dragged on through Friday and Saturday, and there was still no hope of a record and no sign of giving up.

Leo Villa stuck by Campbell of course, and Norris carried on loyally with his graphs and his mathematics. But for the rest of us the Bluebird Project died that week. All that remained was one man with an obsession. It was as sad and as futile as that.

Tonia had the worst of it. For most of us the only real problem was how soon we could get away. For her it was how her husband could be saved without destroying everything he lived for.

It was hard to believe now that this was a record attempt at all. Everything about it was unreal. The world outside had no existence here. All that counted was this solitary madman, a man who had lost hope and lost fear, a man who was fighting himself in this great car he had constructed from his own dreams.

The wind kept up. The long ruts in the track refused to disappear although they had been filled up with loose salt and smoothed countless times with the drags, and it was not until Sunday 7 June that Campbell got his chance.

The previous afternoon he and Norris had met at the lake to

decide what was to be done. Campbell knew that Norris would be flying back to England within forty-eight hours and that the specialist engineers would be following him. But that had not been mentioned. They had taken their time examining the track together—Campbell in his blue Ampol jacket, Norris in an ink-stained gaberdine windcheater buttoned to the neck—and they had not said much, even when they kicked the loose salt crystals packed into the ruts and saw the water still lying on the surface at the intersection with the old main course.

They had driven back to the base camp where Leo Villa was working on the car.

'Tomorrow then, Ken,' Campbell had said. 'Better make it an early start. Seven-thirty all right for you, Unc?'

The old man had nodded.

'And Ken. It'll have to be one hundred per cent power on the turbine. This may be our last chance.'

'I can't advise it, Don. I must warn you what you're going to be up against on that track.'

'Ken, my dear old boy, let's not be silly. We all know what we're up against. But I've got to go and it's not your responsibility any longer. You and Leo have both done your job a hundred times over. Now it's my turn.'

Nothing was said to the rest of us about *Bluebird* running at full power for the first time on Lake Eyre. Gloomily we drove to the lake before light the next morning.

'Another bloody run. Another damned waste of time,' muttered one of the cameramen as we jolted our way through the dark in our Land Rover. 'Christ it's cold. I never knew bloody Australia could be as cold as this.'

Half a mile ahead we could see the bobbing tail-lights of the truck in front. Dust swirled in the long yellow tunnels of our headlights. And as we drew near the lake we saw the first sign of dawn—a thin slice of grey cutting into the darkness of the east.

The wind still blew as Campbell waited by the car, blue tennis shoes in his hand, and the slow rigmarole of the start-up began.

'Is this going to it then, Donald?' asked Parr.

'Perhaps, Wally. Let's just see.'

'Everything all right now with the stewards?'

'Fine. Fine. I'm not worried about the stewards now. It's this wind.' And it kept up, gusting and lapsing then neurotically renewing itself just as there seemed a chance of calm—a fretful, feminine wind that kept promising to change its mind but never did.

So the hours dragged by and the sun glared stronger and the mirage began to dance with the blue guide line where the track met the horizon and *Bluebird* stayed where she was. Even the movie cameras looked as if they had been kept waiting too long. Limbo began.

By midday it looked like yet another day down the drain, and in twos and threes people began to drift into the tent where the sandwiches and the coffee had been left in the big cardboard boxes. Most ate from boredom rather than hunger.

Campbell was one of the last to come in. He stood in one corner with Norris, and neither spoke as they munched their sandwiches. They had nearly finished when Tonia burst in.

'Quickly, Donald,' she shouted. 'It's dropped—the wind's dropped. Come and see, but be quick.'

She was right. The red and yellow Dunlop flag was hugging the pole and the day was suddenly calm. Campbell had his moment after all, and the rush began to get *Bluebird* away while it lasted. Like sleepwalkers who suddenly awake, the *Bluebird* team jerked into action, and it seemed a matter of seconds before the canopy was closed and the exhaust was growling from the car's tail.

There had been so much delay that it was hard to believe this was a full-scale record bid, and that nine years of waiting could still pay off in the next sixty minutes. Timekeepers and stewards were in their places. Movie cameras were lined up for the start, and long-lensed cameras were already straddled on their tripods by the measured mile as *Bluebird* thundered past in the early afternoon.

But there was to be only one run and at the end of it Campbell was sitting in the cockpit, helmet off, hopelessness once again on his face. He spoke to no one until Ken Norris appeared. Then he shook his head and said, 'Sorry, Ken. Everything seems against us. I had my foot right down that time but I was getting only sixty per cent power as I went through the mile. Must be a fault somewhere in the throttle. And the track—it's still no bloody good. She fell back into the old ruts just past the mile. The tyres were locked in for some way, and when they came out the force nearly threw her right off. If I'd had full power then I'd have bought it and no mistake.'

He climbed out of the cockpit and began discussing the fault of the throttle mechanism with Leo Villa. The old man was suddenly at his most energetic—questioning, gesticulating, examining the car. Mechanics clustered round *Bluebird* like doctors at a rich man's death bed.

'That's that,' said Parr. 'If the ruts are still there, there's nothing he can do now.' He looked across at Campbell who was standing on his own, hands deep in pockets, cigarette sloping from the corner of his mouth, staring along the track which had once again come so near to killing him.

'It must be very hard when you decide on death or glory and then don't get the chance of either,' said Parr. 'But it must end now. He'll have to postpone.'

But the wait went on, even then, and somehow a rumour got round that *Bluebird* might be running again that afternoon. The cause of the cut in power was soon discovered—a minute leak in the hydraulic valve belonging to the throttle mechanism—and Carl Noble of Electro Hydraulics was said to be fitting another.

But by four o'clock it was clear that *Bluebird*'s day was over, and Superintendent Brebner took Campbell to one side for the conversation he had been rehearsing in his mind for several days. Before he could begin Campbell said, 'It's all right, Cliff. I know what you're going to say.'

'Well, we can't go on like this, can we, Don? After today you're obviously not going to get anywhere with the track, the way it is, and I don't think my boys can take much more of this waiting around. It's nearly two months now.'

'I know, Cliff, and I'm very grateful. What do you suggest?'

'In my opinion you should postpone now. And quickly, while you've still got the car and everyone's good will. If you hang on much longer I think you'll have real trouble. Leave straight away. Then come back in a couple of months and your track will have hardened if you're lucky. Take my advice. Let the air clear and the salt harden.'

'Okay, Cliff. Thanks for the advice. Can I make up my mind this evening and let you know then?'

As the afternoon ended Campbell must have known his last chance of avoiding a postponement was over. But before committing himself irrevocably he felt he had to talk to Norris.

He found him in his caravan. Books and clothes were piled on the bed, an open suitcase beside them.

'So you're off now, Ken.'

'Sorry, Don, I must get back. The doctors say it'll be in a day or two. I should get back just in time.'

'Don't apologise to me, old boy. I should be making the apologies for keeping you here so long. I'll fly you down to Adelaide first thing tomorrow, so you'll be in good time for the midday plane to Sydney.'

With the mess and muddle of departure the caravan appeared even smaller than usual, and it seemed impossible that three men could have lived in it for so long. Two empty Australian sherry bottles stood in the sink. The film projector was on the floor. There was a smell of eggs and bacon and male clothing. Campbell sat on one of the unmade beds and carefully lit his pipe.

'Ken,' he began. 'I know it's all over.'

Norris stood awkwardly at one end of the caravan. He nodded but said nothing.

'But you know, something happened today, Ken. Something I don't understand.'

Norris pushed the suitcase from the bed then and sat down. Campbell took the pipe from his mouth and leaned forward, elbows on knees, staring intently at him.

'You realise, Ken, I should have been killed today. When those wheels went in the ruts I had my foot down as hard as it would go. If I'd had the hundred per cent power you gave me, she'd have gone right out of control. Instead, at the very moment I'm for the high jump, the one valve in the car that matters decides to leak. You're a rational fellow, Ken. Explain that to me.'

'It could have happened any time, Don. You were just lucky.'

'Lucky be damned. You'll be telling me it was a coincidence next.'

It was after dinner when Campbell called on Brebner at the army camp. He was wearing his old red and white neck scarf and there was some colour back in his face.

'Okay, Cliff,' he said, smiling and opening his hands as if to show that he had nothing left to offer. 'You're right. Absolutely right. We postpone.'

It was stuffy in the tent with the smell of canvas and dust and cigarette smoke. Brebner was sitting on his camp bed. The two lines of his medal ribbon caught the light from the sixty-watt bulb in the centre of the tent. It was he who looked tired now, not Campbell.

'Are you sure this is what you really want, Don? I'd hate you to feel I'm pushing you into it.'

'Thanks, Cliff, but it's my decision. We'll leave the cars here and all the equipment. Leo and the boys can do with a break. So can I. But everything stays where it is, and we come back just as soon as we get word that the lake's ready.'

'You really will be coming back then?' said Brebner slowly.

The question seemed to puzzle Campbell. 'We came here for a record, Cliff. So far we've failed to get it.'

Campbell announced his decision to the rest of the camp later that night at a meeting in the shearers' quarters, and the exodus from Muloorina began next morning as soon as it was light.

It was a cold, windy day with high cloud, and a pair of eagles were circling above the homestead from dawn. There was dust in the air and the great empty land beyond looked grey and devoid of all hope. The circus was folding—noisily, anxiously, with everyone in a hurry and men shouting to each other as they roped bags to roof-racks and checked petrol and water and gathered their belongings for the long drive south.

One by one the cars roared off down the track to Marree, past the whitened piles of camel bones, past the deserted tents, across the creek by the gum trees where Elliot Price had marked out his grave.

At eight-thirty the Aero Commander took off for Adelaide with Ken Norris and some of the engineers aboard. And by afternoon the only evidence left behind by the last two months was the row of empty caravans beyond the shearers' quarters and the hillock of tin cans, not yet rusted, behind the homestead.

The two eagles were still in the sky when Elliot Price came out on to the verandah, yawning from his after-dinner nap. He saw his son-in-law by the barn.

'Well, boy, they've gone,' he shouted. 'Now we can get down to some work.'

He put his thumbs behind his braces and gazed at the empty wilderness he owned.

'It'll be all right, boy'

Nothing had changed. There was no reason why it should have done, but all the way up to Muloorina on that Thursday afternoon five weeks later Campbell had been wondering whether this time it was going to be different. Then he banked the Aero Commander low over the lake and saw the deceptive brown and gold of the salt from five hundred feet and knew that he was simply back where he had left off.

True, some of the people had changed. He had seen to that. There were two new stewards, and he had them with him now in the aircraft—Alec Hawkins, an official of the Melbourne Light Car Club, and Dr Lloyd Buley, deputy chief medical officer of the Department of Civil Aviation. Campbell had taken to them both from the moment they first met in Melbourne, and, unlike their predecessors, they did not seem to feel that their official duties compelled them to keep their distance from Campbell.

Buley, a former RAAF pilot, had lost both legs during the war, but still drove his blue Porsche through the streets of Melbourne and acted as chief medical officer to the Confederation of Australian Motor Sports. A trip to Lake Eyre seemed exactly the sort of outing he enjoyed.

Andrew Mustard was still in charge of *Bluebird*'s tyres and wheels. All his former responsibilities for the track and the project as a whole had been split between Evan Green and Campbell's genial friend, Graham Ferrett, manager of Yorke Motors in Adelaide. And the postponement had inevitably caused casualties among several of *Bluebird*'s key personnel.

Norris, now the proud father of a four-week-old son called Louis-John, was back, and had brought with him George Hammond of Bristol Siddeley and Ron Willies of Girling. Scrimshire and Noble, the two specialist engineers, had not been able to return and Reaks, the expert on *Bluebird*'s instruments, was missing too.

For the truth was that the odds against Campbell winning his record now seemed even bleaker than when he called off the attempt at the beginning of June, and the sight of the lake suddenly revived all his own worst doubts. In those last few minutes before bringing in the Aero Commander to land at Muloorina, he went through them again one by one. There was the salt. Would it really be any harder? And money. How much longer could he keep up the expense of the attempt on his own? Would he find the weather he needed at this time of the year?

During the weeks away from Lake Eyre he had had time to think over his whole future. He knew that he could easily have called off the record attempt for good. Most people seemed to take it for granted that he would, and sometimes even he wondered about it himself.

He and Tonia had travelled together to Sydney for a short holiday and then gone on to Brisbane, and as they picked up their old way of life again Lake Eyre had seemed a long way away and life very much worth living. Several times they talked of settling in Australia—buying a farm or a business and selling the house in Surrey. The country suited them both. They liked the climate and the people and the Australian way of life.

Most of his doubts about returning to Lake Eyre had concerned Tonia. He told himself that it was unfair to ask her to endure the strain of a record attempt all over again.

But during these weeks something had made him go on, and he knew there was really no question of avoiding the return to Lake Eyre. Something told him that this time it would be all right. He remembered how the throttle valve had leaked and saved him from almost certain disaster on that last run. In his career as a record breaker there had been too many escapes like this for them all to be explained by the long, uncertain arm of coincidence. There was a pattern to it all. Someone somewhere must be looking after him.

As he circled Muloorina there seemed to be no sign of life. The caravans were still there beyond the homestead. The tents of the army camp were exactly as he remembered them. There was the big corrugated-iron shed with 'Muloorina' painted in black across the roof, and to the right lay the dull red ribbon of the airstrip.

He looked back at Tonia then put the aircraft down hard, keeping the stick pulled back into his stomach and the nose up until the last possible moment. Only when the two rear wheels touched the runway and the end of the strip came racing towards him did he ease the nose forward and feel the aircraft whirring to a halt. He switched off the motors.

'So you're back after all, Donald,' shouted someone from outside. 'Some of us had our doubts we'd be seeing you again, but we kept your bed aired just in case.'

Campbell opened the side window of the cockpit, and saw Elliot Price standing beside his gleaming black car at the edge of the airstrip. He had the same braces, the same collapsed grey trilby, the same cautious old sheep-farmer's smile.

'Don't worry about the bed,' shouted Campbell. 'Have you managed to do anything to the lake?'

'That's all right, Don,' said Elliot, nodding sagely. 'You'll be surprised what's happened to it while you've been away.'

'How soon d'you think, Unc?'

'Well, Skipper, the car's ready. The timekeepers got up here yesterday. Now the bloody driver's arrived there's nothing between us and the record.'

Leo Villa grinned and looked at Campbell over the top of his spectacles. For the past five days he and his two assistants, Maurie Parfitt and Brian Coppock, had been back at Muloorina working on *Bluebird*. More than ever he felt responsible for Campbell, and would have given anything to have had the record bid take place somewhere else. He did not trust Lake Eyre. He never had from the start. But he knew he must keep these doubts to himself now. Nothing could be allowed to shake Campbell's new mood of optimism.

'But what about the lake, Unc?' asked Campbell. 'Has the track really improved? What about those damned ruts?'

The note of appeal in his voice was familiar to Villa, for over the years he had heard it many times before. He could remember times when young Donald had wanted something forbidden by his father. He had always turned to Leo then, and the old man had learned with experience exactly how to reply—guardedly, conspiratorially, without giving the boy all he wanted, but without refusing him entirely.

'You mustn't go expecting too much, Skipper,' he said now. 'It's still a lousy track. But it's better, just a shade better, than it was.'

'Too late for us to go and have a quick look at it before dark, I suppose?' said Campbell.

'Now take it easy, Donald. There's all tomorrow.'

'But I want to run tomorrow. I tell you, Unc, I don't intend to stay in this place a single minute longer than I have to.'

'You mean it's going to be quick?' said Parr, laughing mirthlessly. 'Really, Ken, you've had more to do with record bids than to talk like that. We could still be here this time next year.' He finished his sherry and wiped his mouth. 'And we probably will be too.'

As usual Norris was drinking bitter lemon. 'No,' he said. 'Just provided we get the weather we need, you'll soon find yourself on the way back to Sydney.'

'How? If you missed the record last time, how do you reckon you're going to get it now? I've had a look at the lake and I can't see much improvement.'

'It's not the lake so much as the car,' said Norris. 'We can increase the power of the turbine. When I was back in England Don asked me to visit the research boys at Bristol Siddeley to see if we couldn't increase the output beyond its hundred per cent rating.'

Parr looked puzzled. 'I don't understand,' he said. 'Surely a hundred per cent is a hundred per cent.'

'Well, the output of a gas turbine is not limited in quite the same way as the output of a piston engine. But for short periods, if you know what you're doing, it's perfectly possible to step up the power beyond its rated capacity.'

'So how much extra power did the research people give you?'

'They said that if it was absolutely necessary we could increase *Bluebird*'s power to a maximum of a hundred and ten per cent.'

'And will you?'

'That's for Don to decide when he's seen the lake for himself.'

There was no question of Campbell's eagerness to get *Bluebird* moving again. First thing next morning—the morning of 10 July— he flew to the lake with Villa and Norris and Evan Green and the cheerful Ferrett. Leo Villa had the car ready for their inspection, jacked up and gleaming inside the hangar.

'Is she okay, Unc?' asked Campbell briefly.

'Never been better, Skipper.'

'Then we'd better have a look at the track. Be nice if we could say the same for that.'

Slowly they drove the length of it from north to south in the big blue Humber. They made a sombre delegation. By now everyone had been deceived by the salt so often that they were wary of making any rash pronouncement.

Campbell was the only one to light a cigarette as they stopped at the measured mile and saw for themselves that the crust of the salt seemed fractionally harder than it had been a month before.

In the distance the big red marker at the start of the mile flapped in the wind and the sun was bright, glaring, like a great arc light which allowed no shadows, no privacy, and as Campbell strolled casually across the track, hands in pockets, occasionally kicking the soft salt with his heel, he was like a condemned man publicly choosing the site of his own execution.

'It's pretty soft, Unc,' he shouted back. 'Not quite what I was hoping for.'

No one replied and his voice sounded small and lost in the great emptiness of the lake.

'But the ruts have hardened over. That's something.'

He walked on, then stopped, took out a blue handkerchief and held it fluttering in the breeze.

'What about this wind?' he shouted. 'The wind, Unc—has it let up at all?'

'No. Seems to be keeping on all the time, Skipper.'

Campbell nodded to himself then, and began to walk slowly back towards the car. As he reached it he put his hand on Norris's shoulder and said, 'Ken, you'd better tell George Hammond that we're going to need that hundred and ten after all.'

All that day the team stood by with *Bluebird* fuelled and timekeepers in their place by the measured mile waiting for the wind to drop. It never did. Nor the day after, nor the day after that.

There was tedium and boredom, but this dawn to dusk standby was never hopeless like the delays and endless disappointments of May.

There were other differences too. Campbell's party was a better unit for survival, and every member knew what to expect. The battles that had gone on within the project had burned themselves out, and instead of being disappointed with each failure, his people were in a mood to be grateful for the smallest success.

This was just as well, for by Sunday night, after three days of waiting, the wind was blowing as strong as ever and the weather forecast promised more to come. Rain was said to be on the way.

At dinner everyone made an effort to keep his doubts to himself, and Campbell announced that if the forecast was right he would fly the two timekeepers down to Adelaide next day and bring back replacements.

Monday the thirteenth dawned bright and windy as ever. Shortly after breakfast Campbell and Norris went for a stroll from the homestead towards the army camp.

'How long will you be away in Adelaide then, Don?' asked Norris.

'Only one night. I'm taking Tonia down with me. She'll enjoy the ride. The two new timekeepers should be getting in from Melbourne tomorrow morning, so you can expect us back in the afternoon.'

They passed Elliot's hens in the chicken run beyond the homestead. Several of the birds were in moult and they perched, melancholy, stranded creatures, sheltering their nakedness behind an old packing case for Stork margarine. Some of their feathers had stuck to the wire netting like tufts of grimy cotton-wool. Others were being blown across the yard on the wind.

'Ken,' said Campbell, 'you are happy about the car now aren't you?'

'Sure, Don. As far as we've gone she seems to have behaved perfectly. But there's still one hell of a lot I'd like to know about the higher speed range. When you feel like giving me the rest of those test runs you promised me I'll have a clearer answer for you.'

'Sorry, Ken, no time for test runs now. You must make do with the data you've got. I'm just waiting now for that one chance I need. Just one. And when it comes, *when* it comes, Ken…' He paused to emphasise what he was saying, and the Price washing flapped behind him. 'I'll take it and gamble everything on it. I don't like gambling but it's the only way now.'

That night, while Campbell slept in Adelaide, rain came once more to Lake Eyre. The next morning Villa and Norris drove out to inspect the track and found the southern end flooded, bringing the total length down to a mere ten and a half miles. The rest of the course was wet, the surface softened.

'My lord, Ken,' said Villa incredulously as he looked along the track. 'The Skipper's had it. We're right back at the bloody beginning again.'

They telephoned the news to Adelaide as soon as they got back to the homestead. Campbell took it philosophically, as he had learned to take most things by now.

'It could take another month to dry out,' said Villa.

'If it does it does, Unc. I'll fly back straight away. What about the timekeepers? No point in bringing them all the way to Muloorina now I suppose?'

'None at all, Skipper.'

'Okay, Unc. I'll send them back to Melbourne. And I think I'll leave Tonia down here for a few days with Florence. You can expect me back this afternoon.'

It took longer for Campbell to get airborne from Adelaide than he had expected, and longer still to make the long flight back to Muloorina. So it was nearly dark when he arrived and there was no time for him to visit the lake.

Not that there seemed any great need for him to do so. The facts were inescapable, and enough of his people had seen the effect of the rain to tell him about it when he held a small meeting that night after dinner. Villa was there and Mustard and Norris and the stewards, and all said the same thing. The three miles of the southern end of the track was completely unusable, and the rest of the course would take at least another month to dry.

'Another postponement then, gentlemen?' Campbell asked grimly.

There was a pause before Norris spoke. 'There's just a chance,

Don, that the rain has softened only the very surface of the track. The core of the salt underneath was pretty hard before the rain. You may find that it's stood up to it better than any of us think.'

Next morning Campbell flew to the lake to see the damage for himself. He landed near the stewards' tent at the northern end of the course. Norris and Villa were with him, and when they checked the course they found the salt harder than anyone had dared to hope.

The southern end was still under water, and a mile or so at the north was damp, but the centre appeared to have dried.

'Well, what d'you think, Unc?' asked Campbell, stamping on the salt with his heel. 'Will it or won't it?'

'Hard to tell, Skipper. Ken could be right about that core of salt below the surface. It's dried far better than I ever thought it could. In a few days we might know the answer.'

'Few days be damned,' said Campbell. 'I'm finding out now.'

Campbell's spur-of-the-moment decision to drive *Bluebird* and settle the question once and for all was typical of him.

At 260 mph *Bluebird* was dead on course, so he applied the full hundred and ten per cent power of his newly rated turbine. The effect was phenomenal. In a matter of seconds his air-speed indicator shot up to three hundred and twenty miles an hour, and he had to bring the speed down because he could feel the cross wind already carrying *Bluebird* to one side of the course.

After the run the team examined the track and found that the car had cut faint ruts in the salt, but conditions were infinitely better than they had expected.

'Well, Unc,' said Campbell just before he flew back to Muloorina, 'it looks as if we'd better get those timekeepers back after all.'

That same afternoon Campbell returned to Adelaide for Tonia and the timekeepers, and they were all back at Muloorina on the morning of Thursday the sixteenth. He was convinced now that his great chance was near and had the whole team standing by at the lake for the rest of the day. But evening came without the wind abating. Campbell seemed quite unconcerned.

'Early start again tomorrow I'm afraid, Unc,' he said, 'but this will be the last of them. I'd like to have her rolling by seven.'

'But what about this bloody wind, Skipper?'

'The wind will be all right. The weather forecast says there'll be a period of calm, and there's damn well got to be. We've all put up with Lake Eyre long enough. Tomorrow's got to be the day.'

'You know it's a Friday, don't you?' he said.

'I don't care what tomorrow is, Unc, as long as it's the day we get the record. And Ken, one hundred and ten per cent power.'

Norris nodded and looked steadily at him. 'One hundred and ten, Don.'

'You realise it's going to be very close,' said Norris. 'The salt's far from ideal still, and once you're over three fifty you're going to have your work cut out to stop those wheels spinning. So take her up to three fifty at full throttle and then ease your foot back just a shade. You'll carry on accelerating, and that should take you through the mile at just over four hundred.'

It was 7.10 on the morning of Friday 17 July, and Campbell had just landed on the lake. For the first time since his return to Muloorina the wind had died away, and he was anxious to be off. The timekeepers had been in position for half an hour, the stewards were ready, the mechanics had completed their final check. It was cold and the salt underfoot felt like ice.

After his brief discussion with Norris, Campbell glanced towards the stewards' tent where the two red Dunlop flags hung motionless against the aluminium masts. Then without a word he took his helmet and his bear and his blue tennis shoes from Tonia and the start-up began.

'Unc,' he said before the canopy closed. 'I know it's Friday, but

I'd just like you to make sure we don't start at seven-thirteen. Seven-twenty's a good round number.'

Norris and Villa took the grey Valiant and raced ahead of *Bluebird* up the side road, so that they saw the car streak past them like a blue rocket and heard the timekeeper's announcement over the car radio before they reached the end of the track.

'The speed through the measured mile was four zero three miles an hour exactly.'

The car was swung round then. Campbell, grim-faced, silent, sat in the cockpit steering as the rest of the team pushed her backwards and forwards in a series of shallow arcs until *Bluebird*'s nose was facing the way it had just come. Then the rams went down, the car raised herself up, and the wheels were changed. Thirty-eight minutes after *Bluebird* had come to rest, she was ready to go again.

The atmosphere was tenser than it had ever been. There was nothing that anyone, not even Villa, could say now. However certain it might seem that Campbell was going to kill himself if he went on, no one could tell him to stop. Instinctively one tries to prevent a man committing suicide, but here this was an instinct that everyone was having to fight down.

Campbell seemed to understand this himself, for we left him then and he waited in the cockpit, silent, completely alone, for the last few minutes to tick by.

Norris was one of the few people who saw what happened. He was standing by the cockpit, and noticed that Campbell was suddenly staring up at the perspex canopy in front of him. All the tension and strain seemed to have gone from his face. His eyes were open very wide. Then he suddenly took a deep breath, shut his eyes and seemed to relax.

He stayed like this for a few seconds, his head on his chest. Then Leo Villa shouted from the booster truck, 'We're okay, Skipper. Ready when you are,' and Campbell opened his eyes and called back, 'Fine, Leo.' The return run had started.

For Campbell it must have been a terrifying journey. The track disintegrated at the third-mile mark, and he felt the wheels go through the surface of the salt. Any other time he would have taken his foot off the throttle, but now there was no going back and his foot stayed where it was on one hundred and ten per cent power. The car began to vibrate as the razor-sharp salt began shredding rubber from the tyres, and when he passed through the measured mile he had no idea whether he had made it or not.

He imagined not, for he was certain that the battering the car was getting from the salt must be slowing it down, and when the run was over and he lifted the canopy he sat there feeling more dejected that he had ever felt in his life before.

It was one of Brebner's policemen who reached him first.

'Well done, Don, you've made it. Four hundred and three.'

'Don't be stupid,' said Campbell. 'That was the first run. Find out what the real speed was. Not that it matters,' he added.

Evan Green and Norris came up then.

'Sorry, chums,' said Campbell. 'We missed it. Our last chance on this track, and we missed it.'

But then the policeman was back. He was shouting now and waving his arms excitedly.

'It *is* four hundred and three. I've checked with the time-keepers. Four hundred and three exactly each way. It's the record, Don.'

Campbell smiled, took off his helmet, and hoisted himself on the back of the cockpit. Somebody cheered, and the small crowd of people who had gathered round the car bore him away on their shoulders.

There was a barbecue that night by the army camp, and although Florence was still in Adelaide they brought her bottles of Great Western champagne out of the ice-box and added a lot of others to them, and by nine o'clock the geese and the pelicans and the rest of the birds along the creek were beginning to object to the noise.

It was a considerable party. Elliot Price was serving the drinks.

The cameramen were feeling very pleased with themselves because they had finally finished their film. And happiest of all the party-goers were several car loads of people from Marree most of us had never seen before.

Soon people were dancing. More wood was thrown on the fire, immense shadows flickered and the night air was sweet with the tang of the woodsmoke.

As a party the only strange thing about it was that it seemed to have so little to do with the people in whose honour it was held. Villa and Norris were there, but they remained very much on the edge of things, and when Campbell finally arrived the party was already going with such a swing that no one seemed to notice him. He looked tired and lost and rather unhappy, and stood watching the party as if he could hardly understand what it was all about.

Elliot Price caught sight of him and came over to shake his hand.

'Well, Don, you've done it. I always knew you would. You've beaten Lake Eyre.'

Campbell looked puzzled, then smiled tolerantly. 'I suppose so, Elliot. Can't quite believe it. Still feel a bit lost, to tell you the truth. But thanks for everything. You've been wonderful, Elliot. I'm very grateful.' He shook hands again, and then walked over to Norris and Villa.

'Always the same, Skipper,' said Villa. 'The more of a struggle to win a bloody record, the more of a let-down when you've got it. I still can't believe in this one.'

Campbell shook his head. 'Nor can I, Unc. It's all over now. Let's forget it. I wanted to talk to you about the water record. The old boat's down in store in Adelaide. She's ten years old but I reckon she's still got a few extra miles an hour in her before we shove her in the museum. How's about getting on with it? No one's ever done the land and the water in one year.'

For the next twenty minutes they talked, planning how they could win the water record—the choice of lakes, the transport problems, the supply of spares and food and fuel. Such talk seemed to bring the three men back to reality, and Campbell was about to leave the party when Norris asked him the question that had been puzzling him all day.

'Don,' he said, 'what happened this morning?'

'What d'you mean, Ken? When?'

'Between the two runs. When you were sitting there in the cockpit waiting for the start, something happened to you, didn't it?'

There was a long pause. 'Yes, old chum,' said Campbell at last. 'Something did happen. It was the most incredible thing I've ever experienced. You know what happened on that first run?'

Norris nodded.

'I nearly killed myself. I was so near to going out of control that it wasn't even funny, and when I was sitting in the cockpit at the end of the run I really thought I had had it. For I knew the second run would be worse. I saw no hope at all.

'It was then that it was so extraordinary. You know how the canopy lifts up with the windscreen in front of the cockpit? Well, I suddenly looked up into it and there was my father reflected in the windscreen as clearly as you're sitting there now. I even recognised the white shirt and flannels he used to wear. For a few seconds he just looked at me, smiling. Then he said, "Well, boy. Now you know how *I* felt that time at Utah when the wheel caught fire in 1935. But don't worry," he added, "it'll be all right, boy."

'Then he faded away.'

Someone threw fresh branches on the fire, and as the smoke billowed up Campbell started coughing. It was probably the smoke that made his eyes water too. He looked across at Villa, whose face had grown wise and golden and timeless in the firelight.

'There never was anyone like the old man, was there, Unc?' he said.

'No,' replied Villa softly. 'No one.'